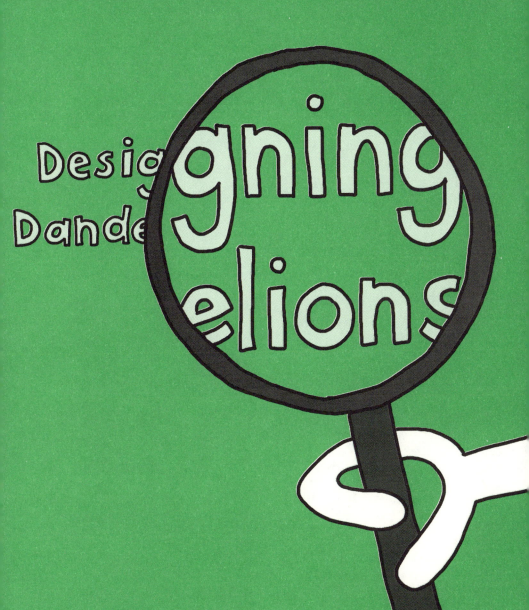

Designing Dandelions

AN ENGINEERING EVERYTHING ADVENTURE

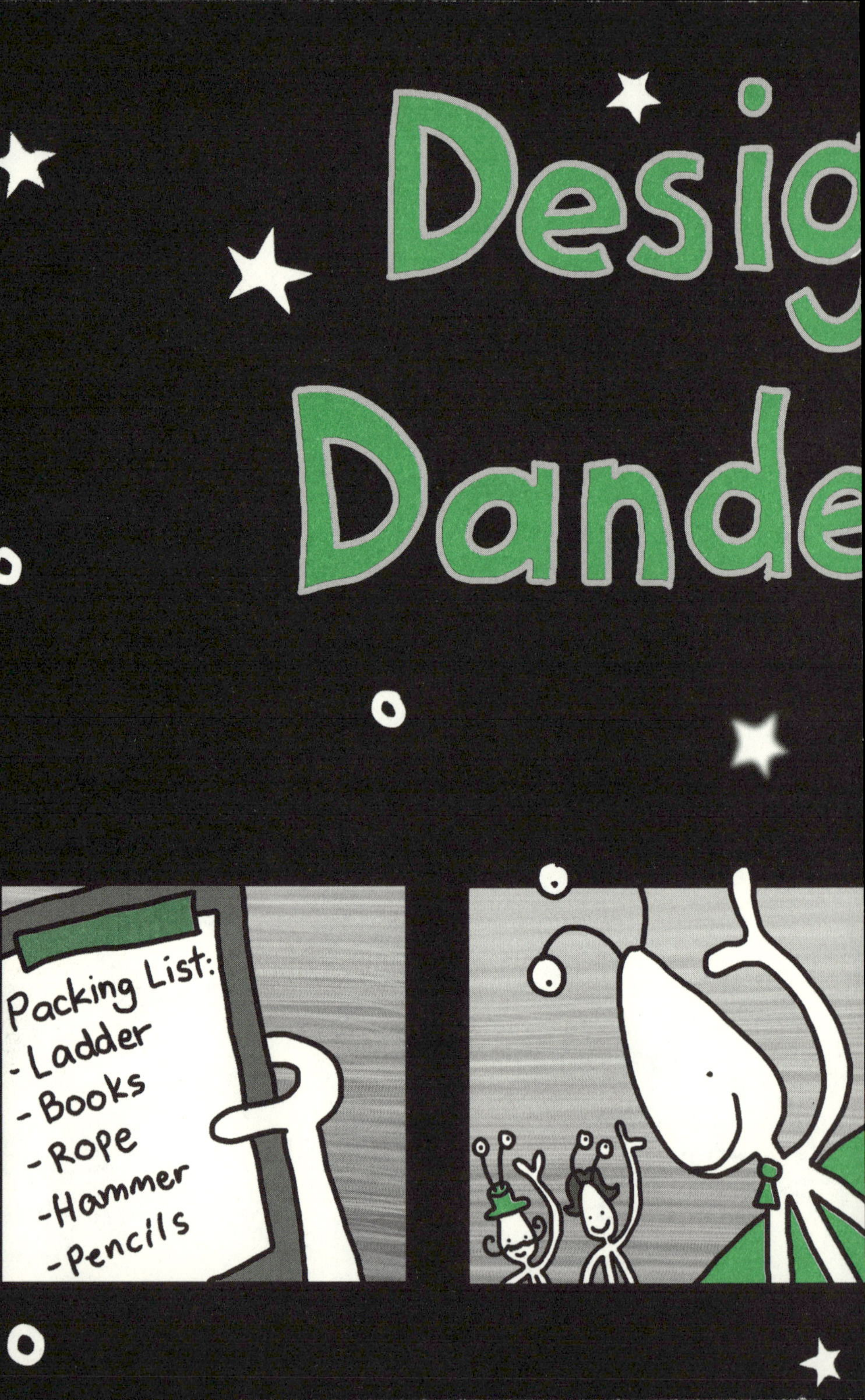
Desig
Dande
Packing List:
-Ladder
-Books
-Rope
-Hammer
-Pencils

hing

ions

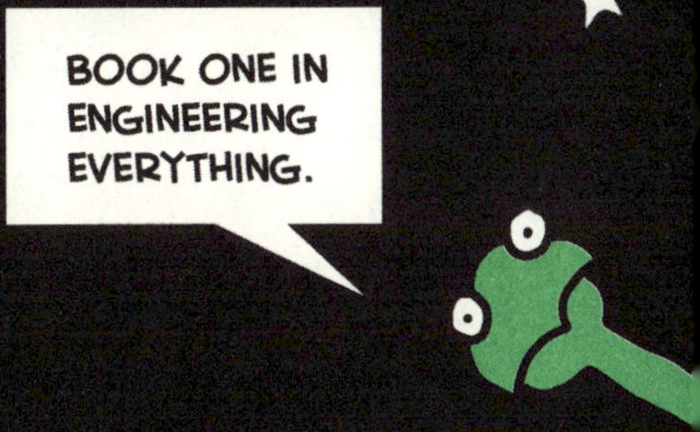
BOOK ONE IN
ENGINEERING
EVERYTHING.

EMILY HUNT AND MICHELLE PANTOYA

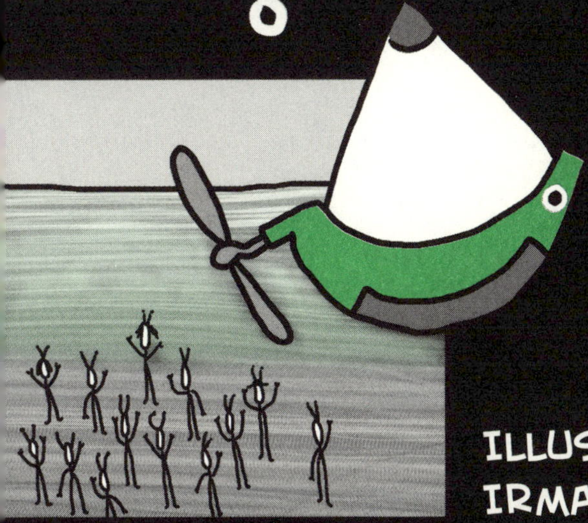

ILLUSTRATED BY
IRMA SIZER

TEXAS TECH UNIVERSITY PRESS

THIS BOOK IS TYPESET IN CREATIVEBLOCK BB.
THE PAPER USED IN THIS BOOK MEETS THE MINIMUM REQUIREMENTS OF ANSI/NISO Z39.48-1992 (R1997). ∞

LIBRARY OF CONGRESS CONTROL NUMBER: 2013938821
ISBN (CLOTH, LITHO CASE): 978-0-89672-849-3

PRINTED IN THE UNITED STATES OF AMERICA
13 14 15 16 17 18 19 20 21 / 9 8 7 6 5 4 3 2 1

TEXAS TECH UNIVERSITY PRESS
BOX 41037
LUBBOCK, TEXAS 79409-1037 USA
800.832.4042
TTUP@TTU.EDU
WWW.TTUPRESS.ORG

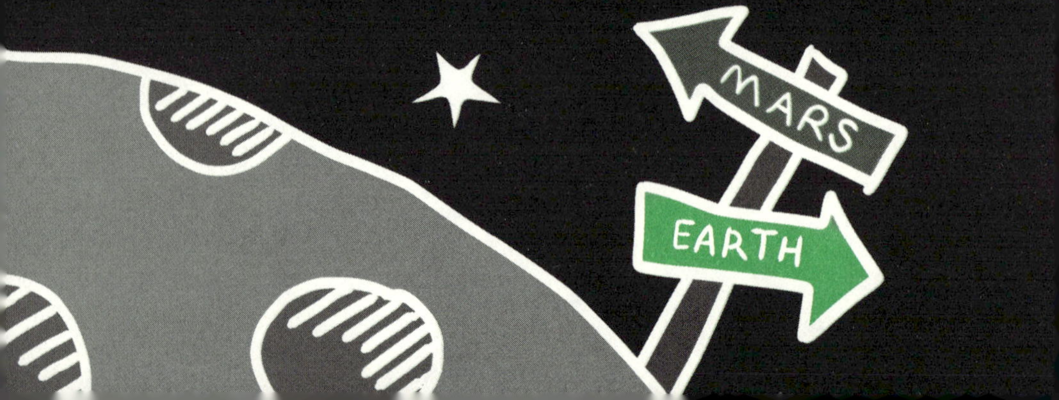
MARS
EARTH

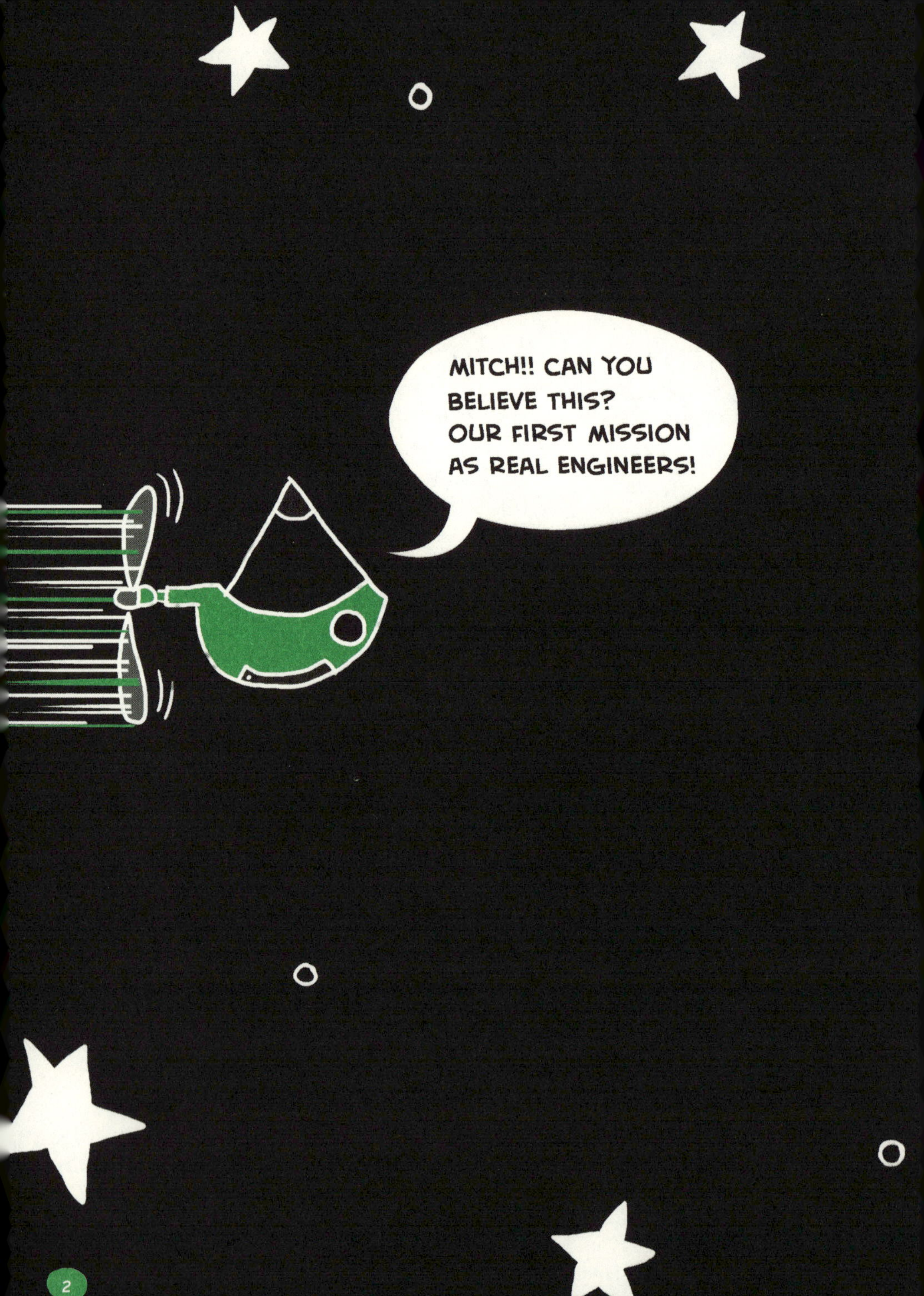
MITCH!! CAN YOU BELIEVE THIS? OUR FIRST MISSION AS REAL ENGINEERS!

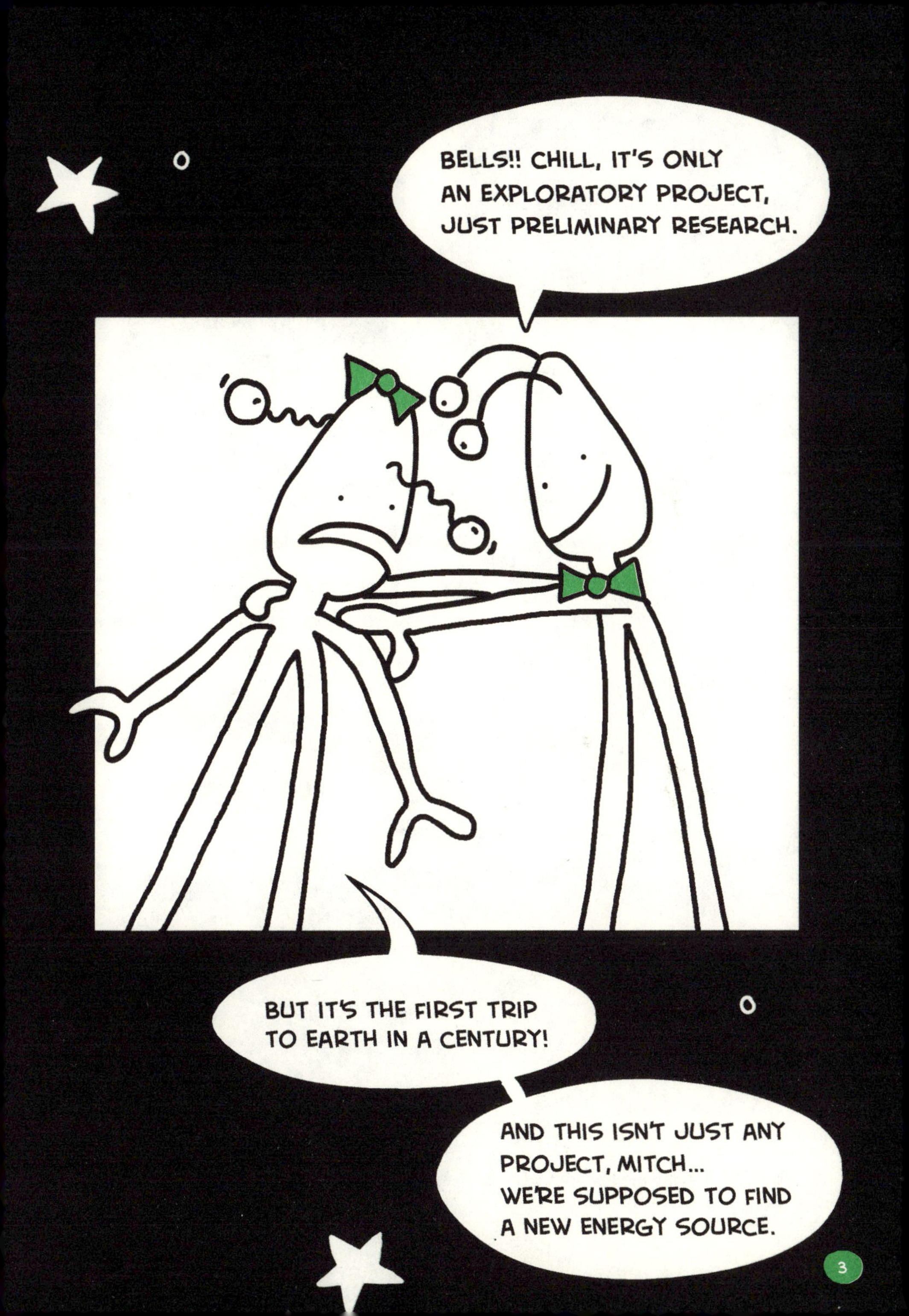

BELLS!! CHILL, IT'S ONLY AN EXPLORATORY PROJECT, JUST PRELIMINARY RESEARCH.
BUT IT'S THE FIRST TRIP TO EARTH IN A CENTURY!
AND THIS ISN'T JUST ANY PROJECT, MITCH... WE'RE SUPPOSED TO FIND A NEW ENERGY SOURCE.

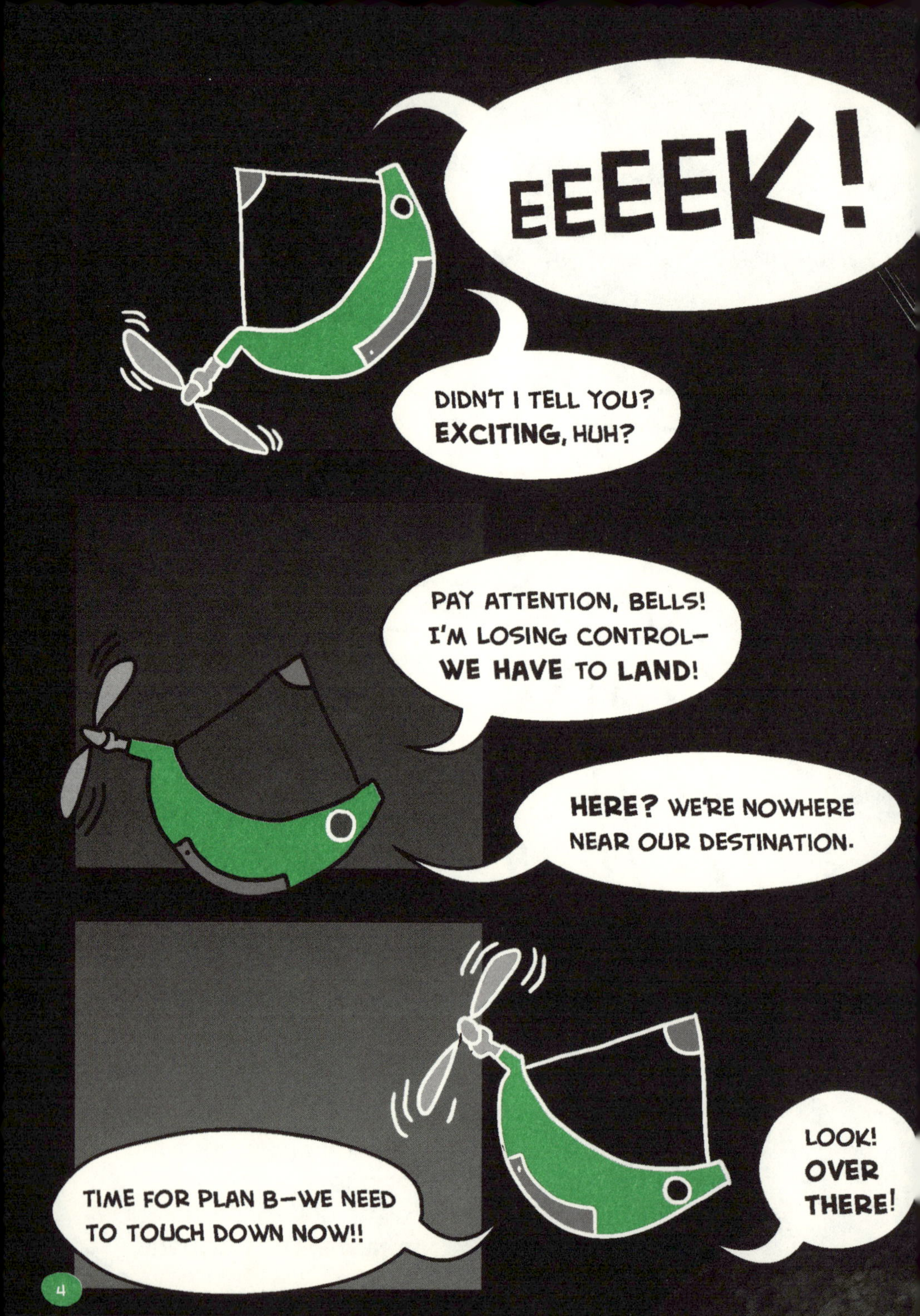
EEEEK!
DIDN'T I TELL YOU? EXCITING, HUH?
PAY ATTENTION, BELLS! I'M LOSING CONTROL— WE HAVE TO LAND!
HERE? WE'RE NOWHERE NEAR OUR DESTINATION.
TIME FOR PLAN B—WE NEED TO TOUCH DOWN NOW!!
LOOK! OVER THERE!

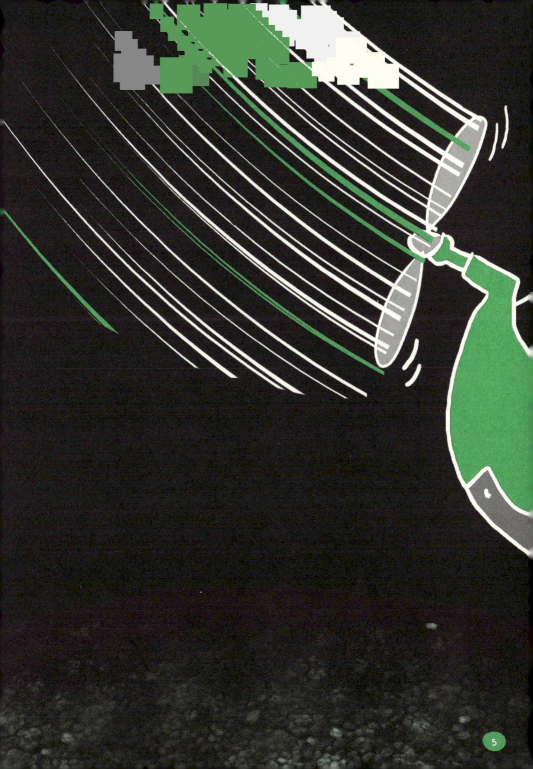

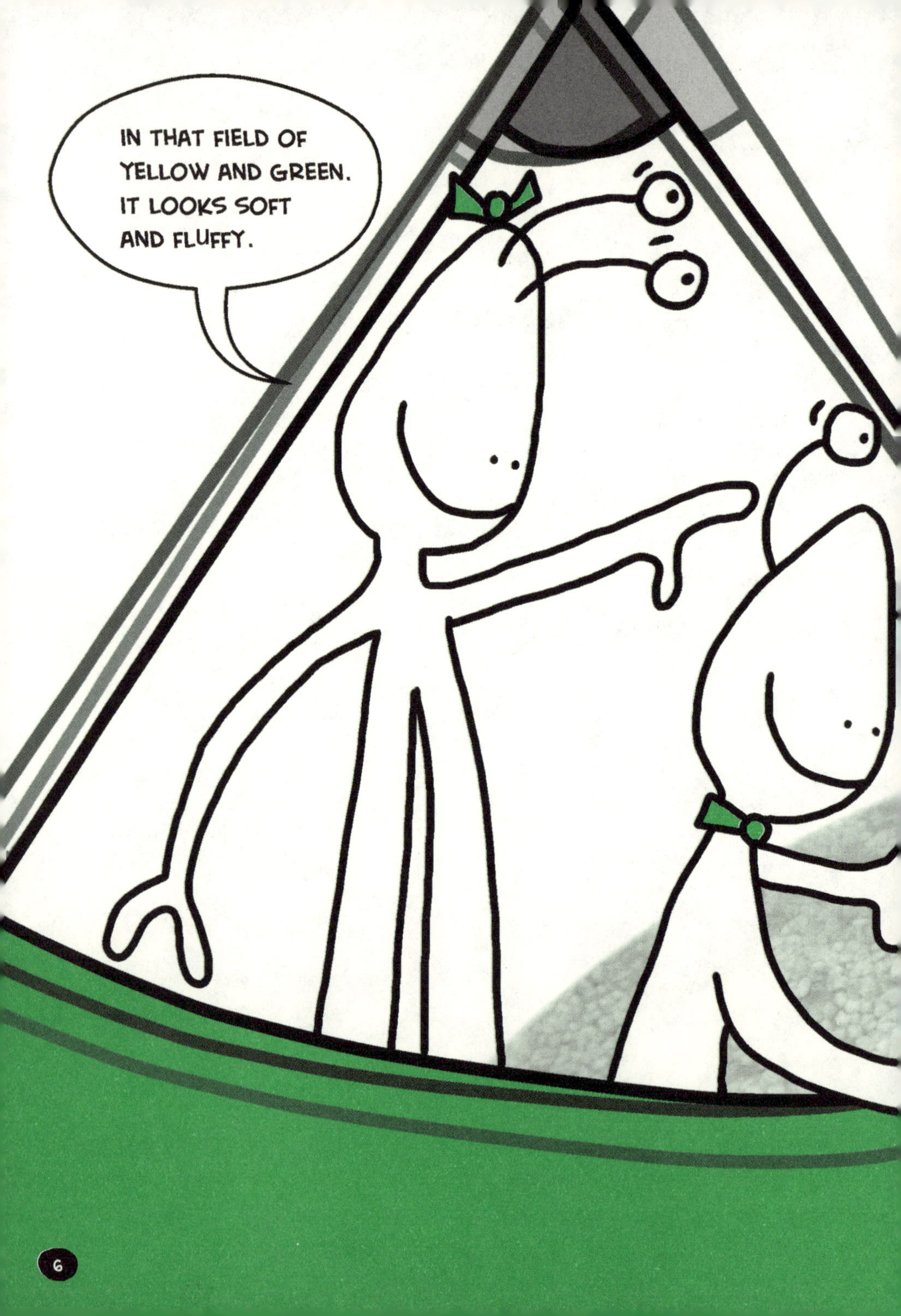
IN THAT FIELD OF YELLOW AND GREEN. IT LOOKS SOFT AND FLUFFY.

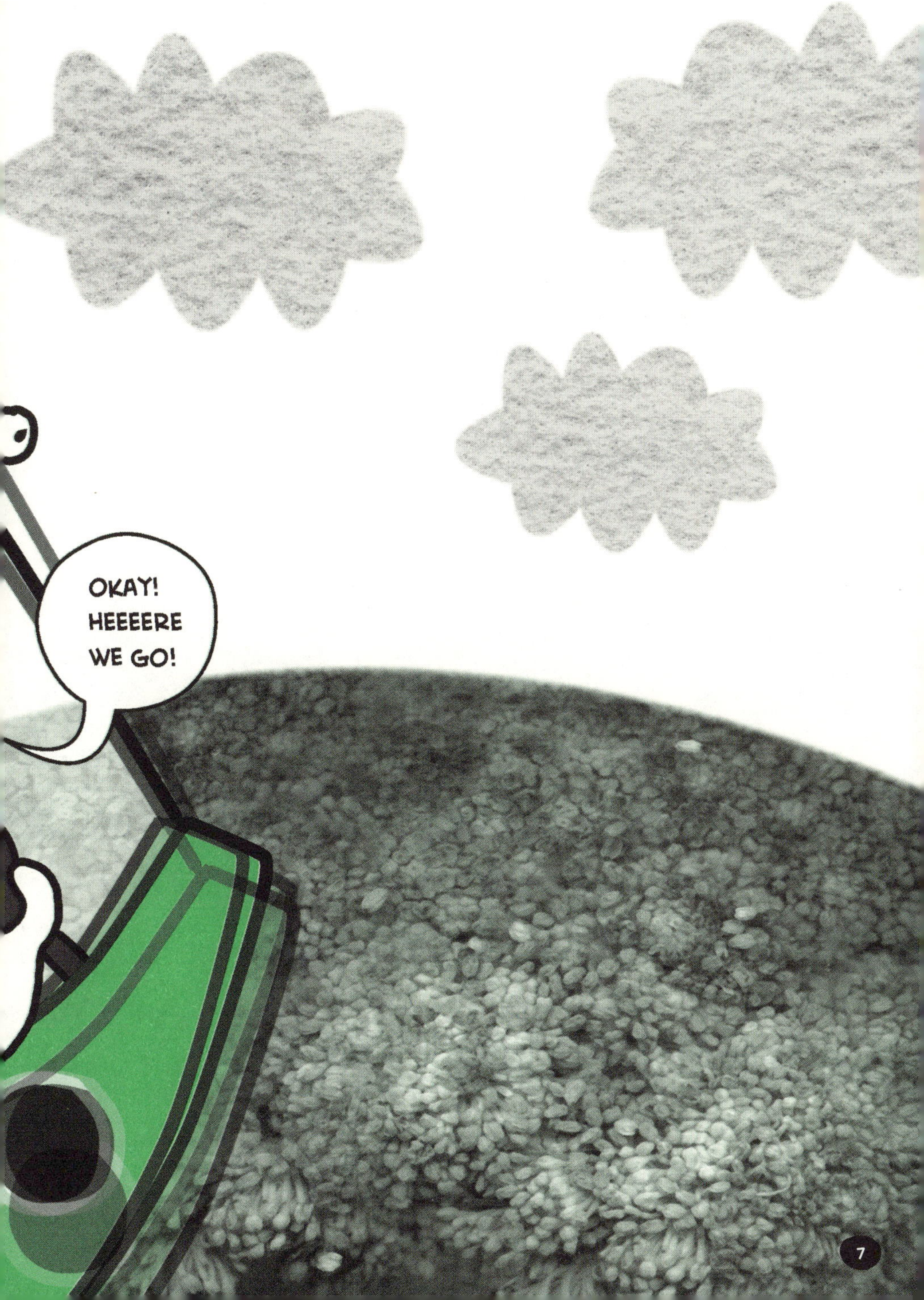
OKAY! HEEEERE WE GO!

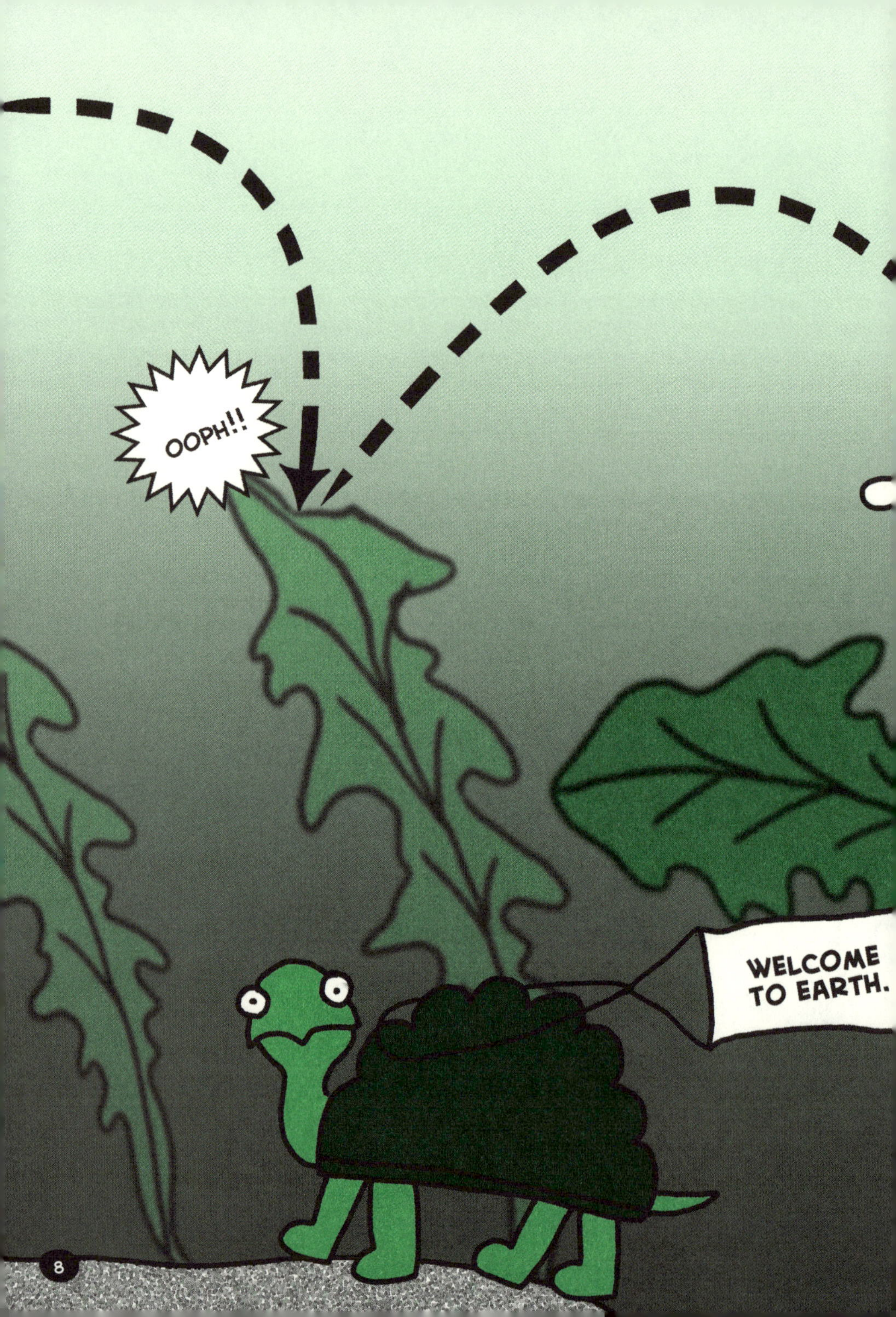
OOPH!!
WELCOME TO EARTH.

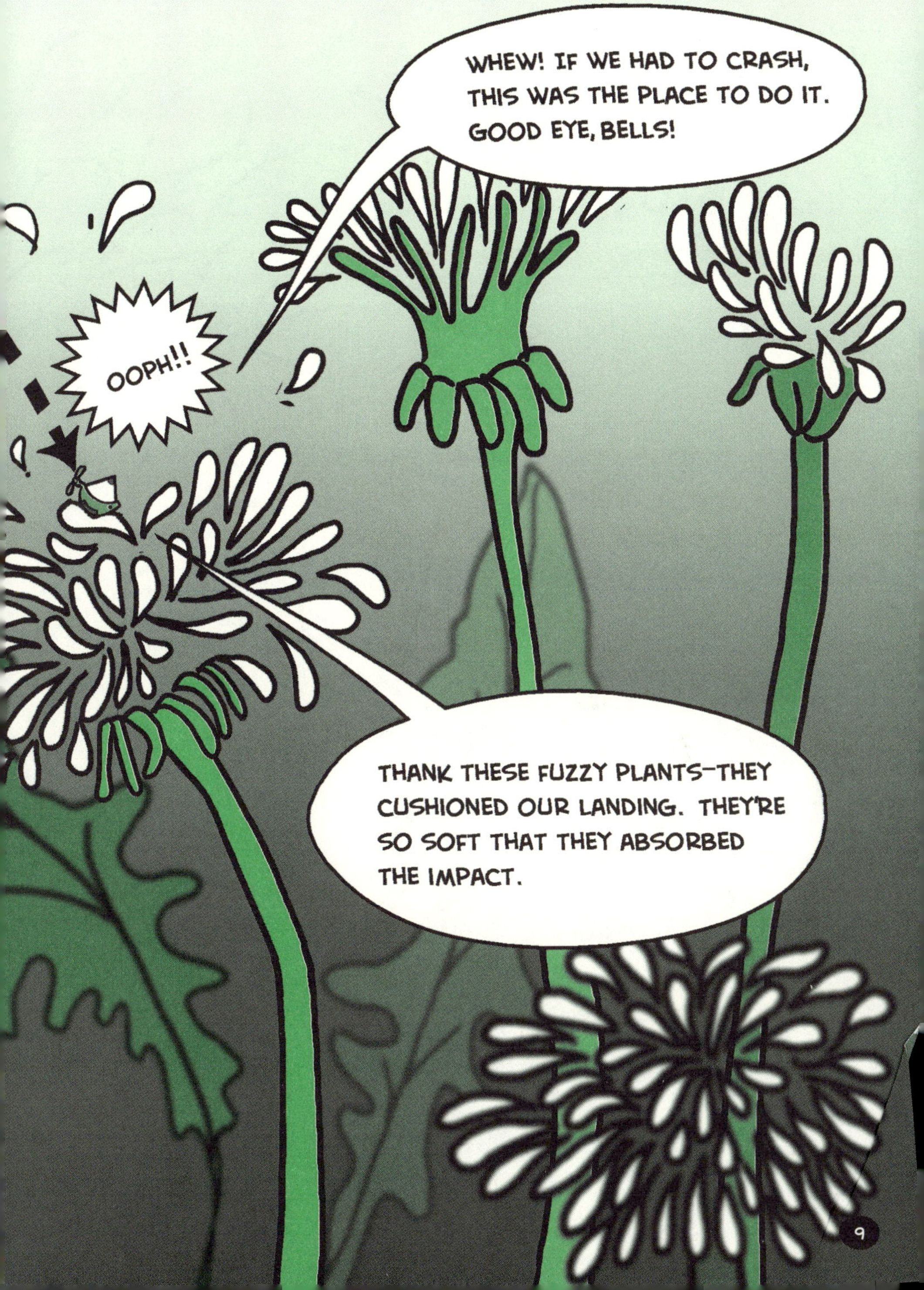
WHEW! IF WE HAD TO CRASH, THIS WAS THE PLACE TO DO IT. GOOD EYE, BELLS!
OOPH!!
THANK THESE FUZZY PLANTS—THEY CUSHIONED OUR LANDING. THEY'RE SO SOFT THAT THEY ABSORBED THE IMPACT.

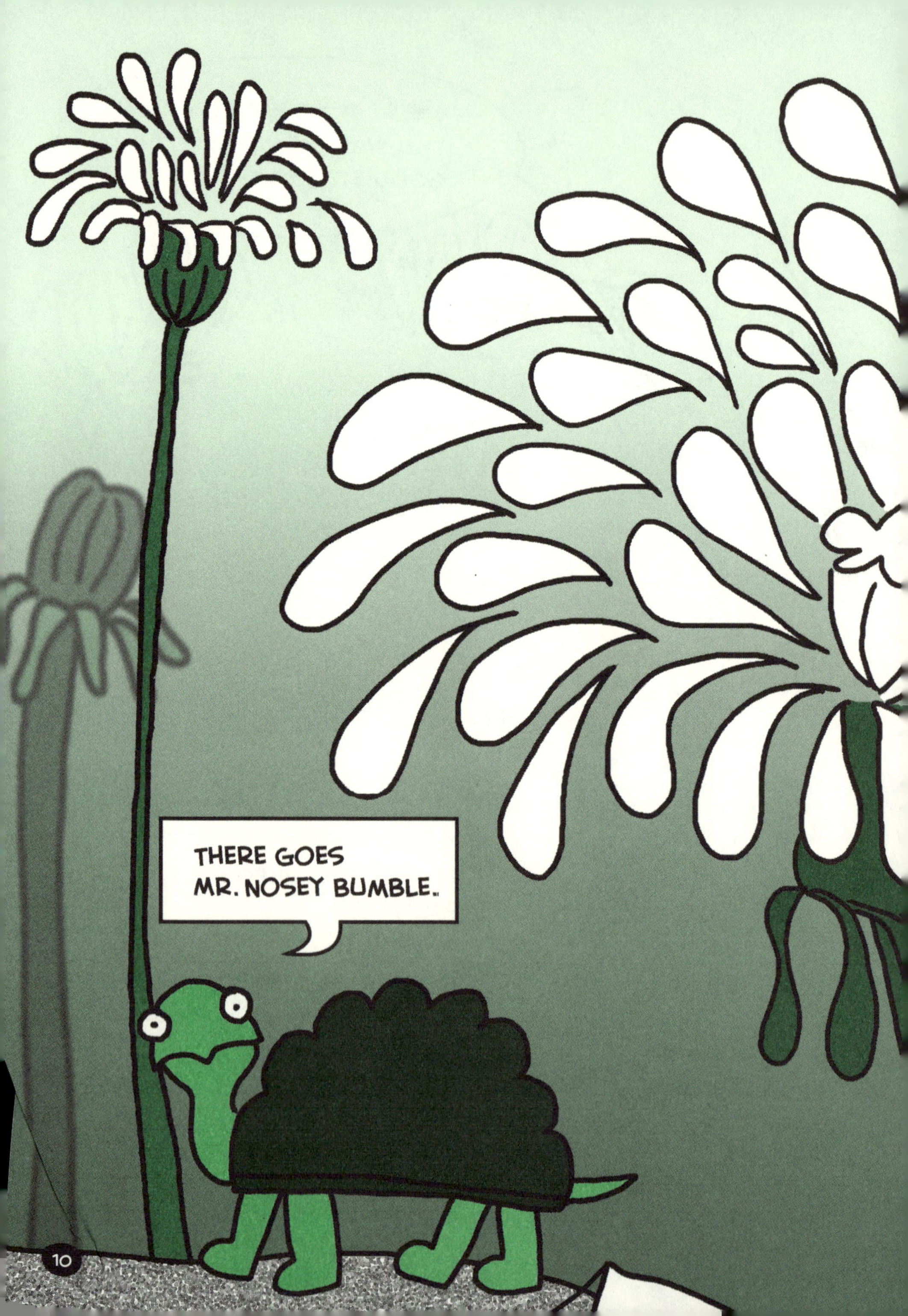
THERE GOES MR. NOSEY BUMBLE..

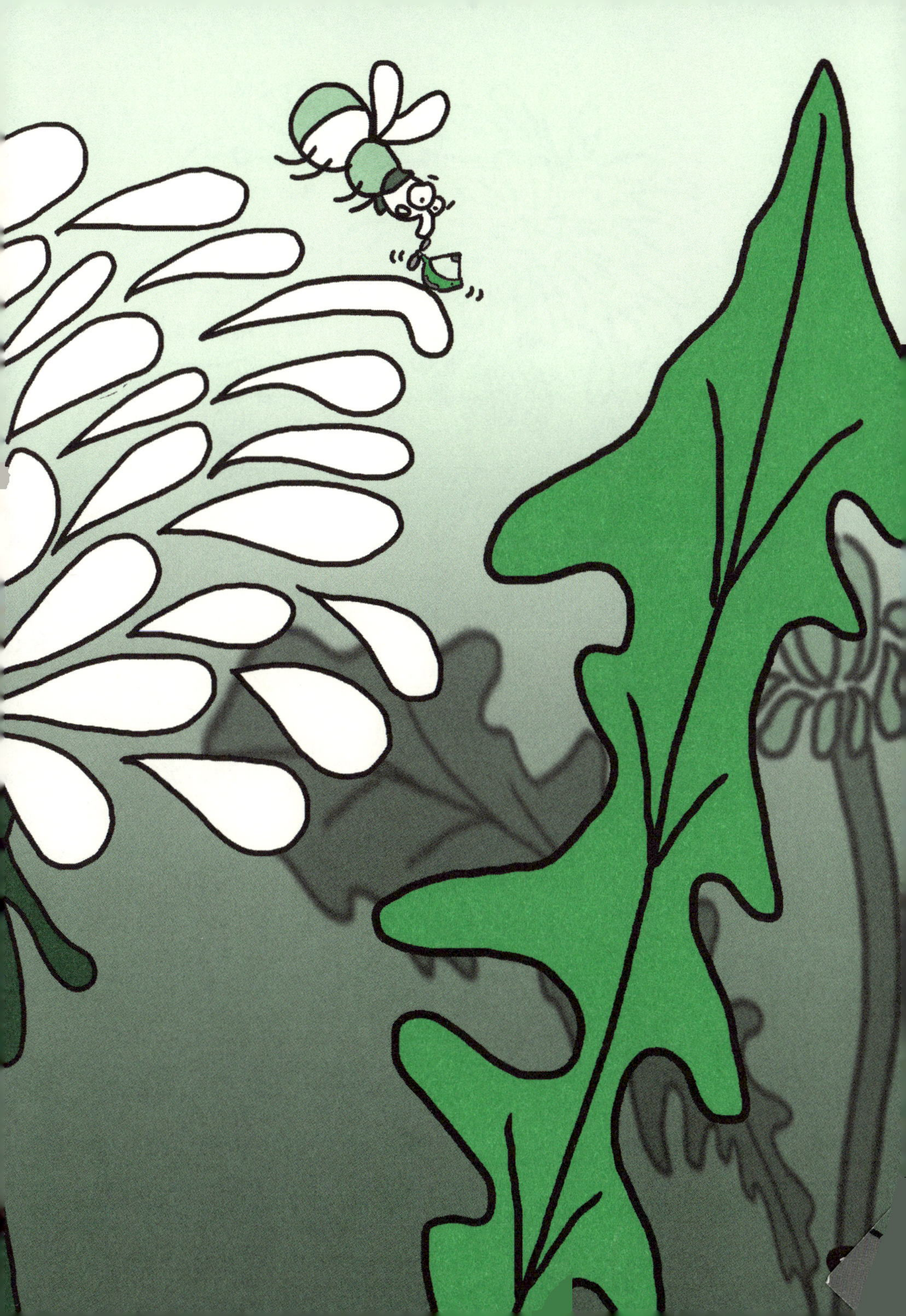

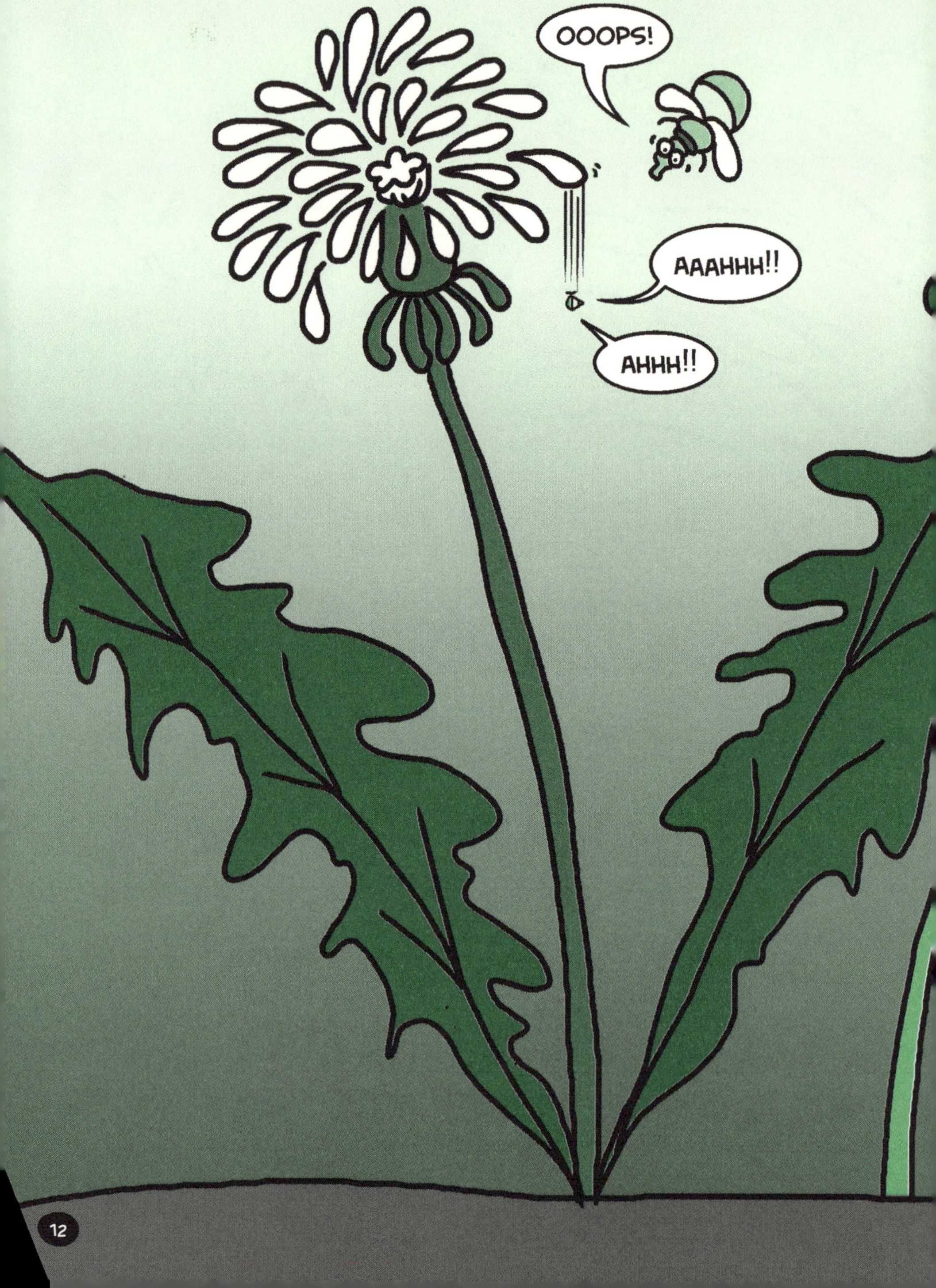
OOOPS!
AAAHHH!!
AHHH!!

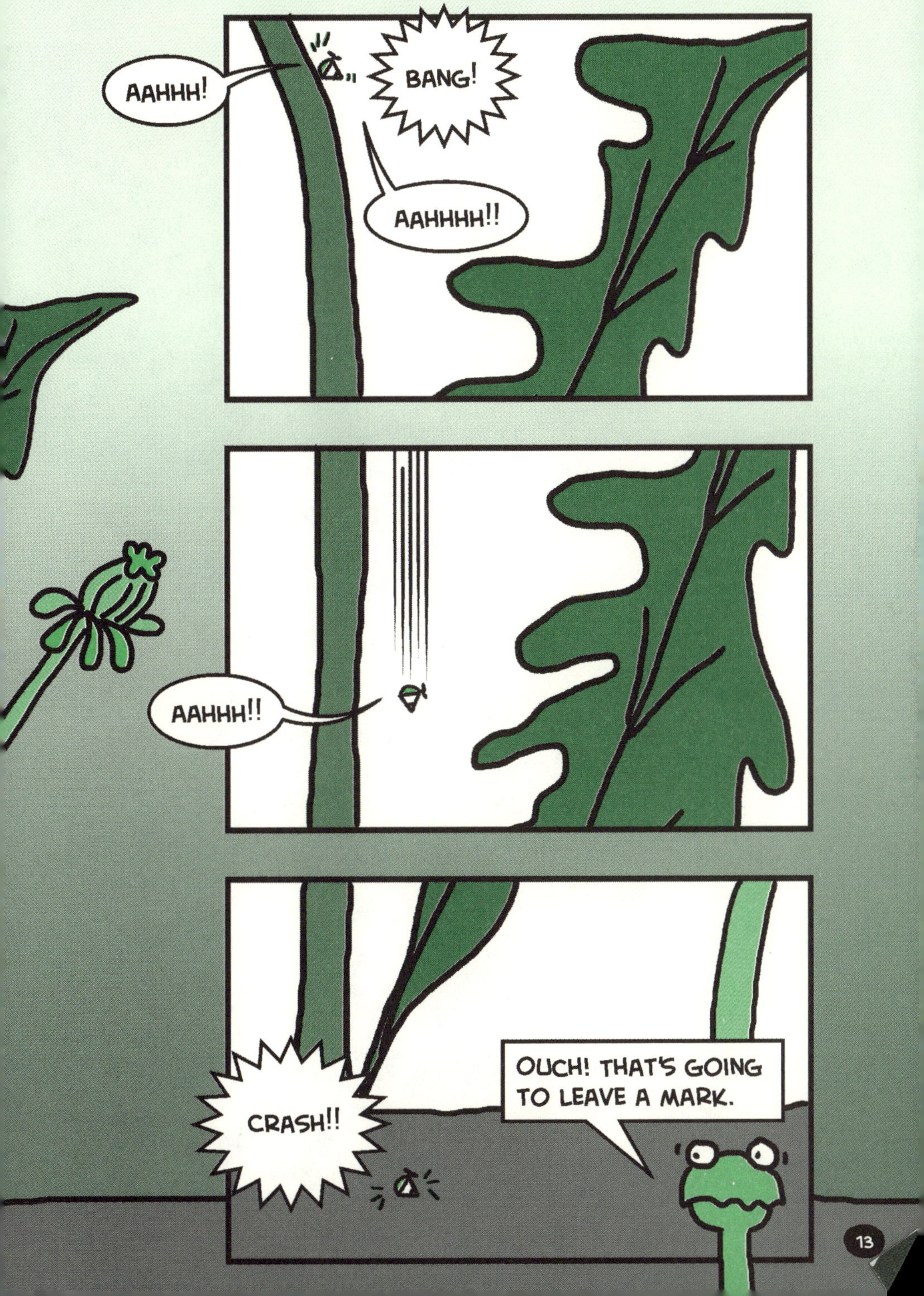
AAHHH!
BANG!
AAHHHH!!
AAHHH!!
CRASH!!
OUCH! THAT'S GOING TO LEAVE A MARK.

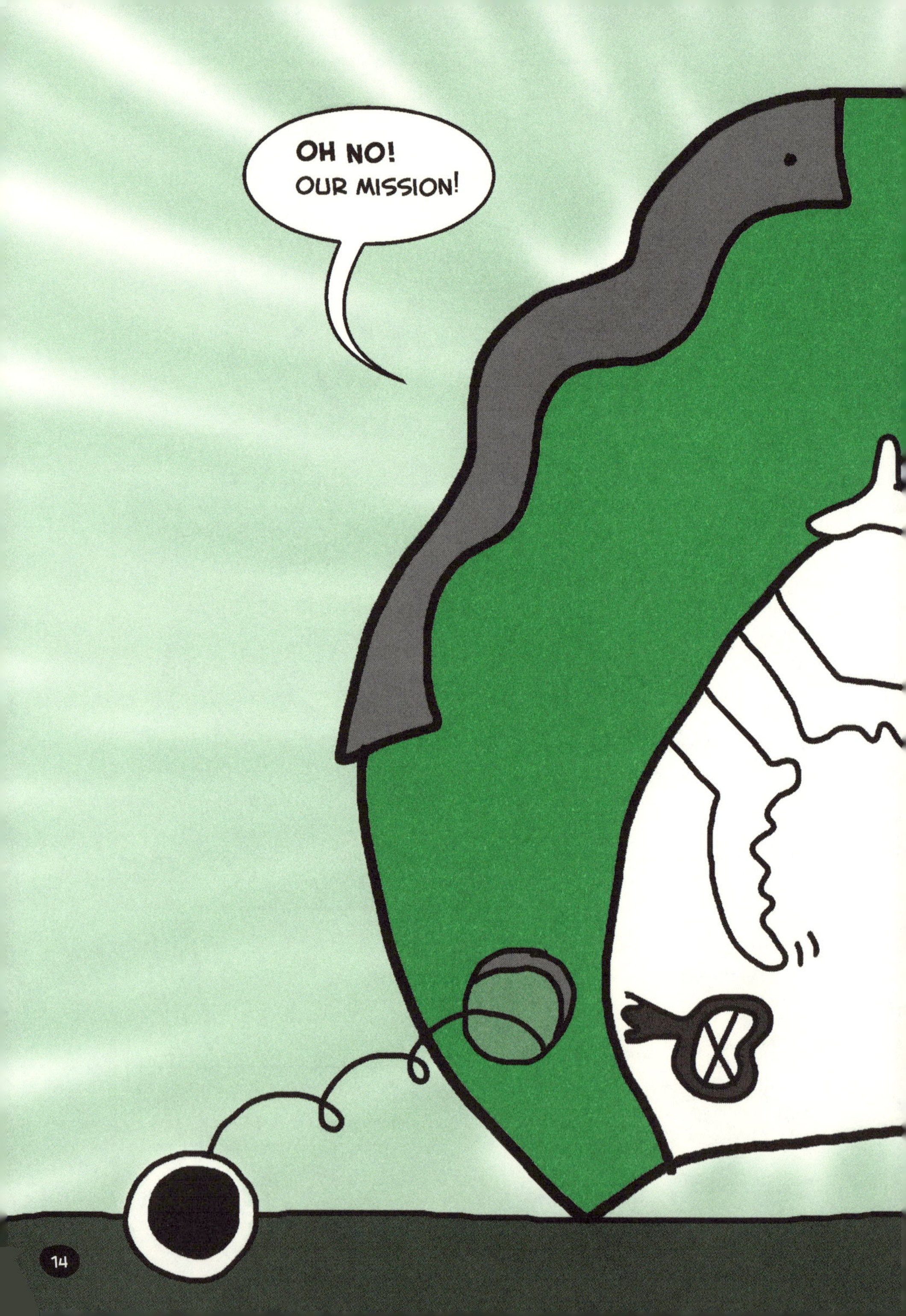
OH NO!
OUR MISSION!

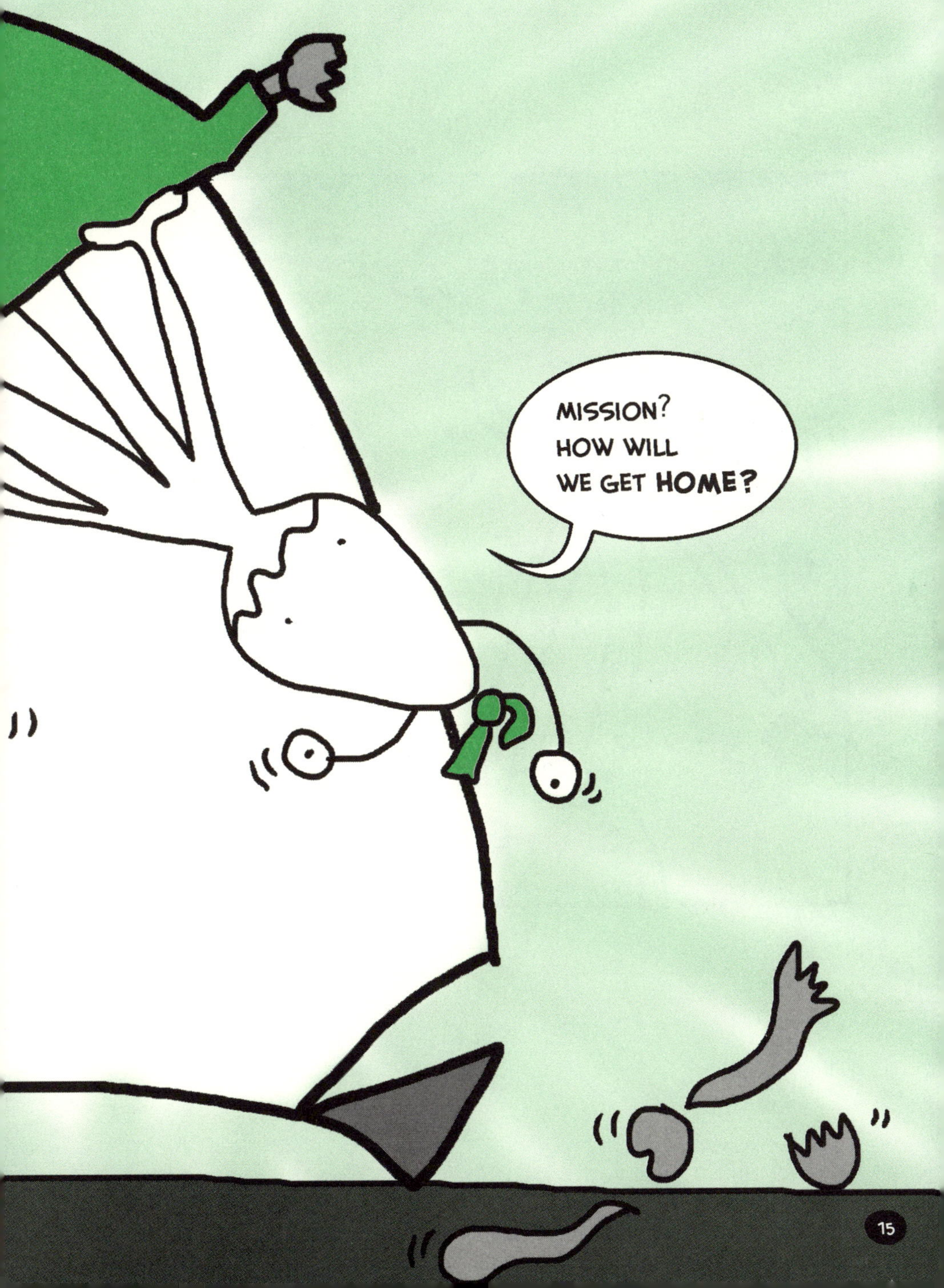
MISSION? HOW WILL WE GET HOME?

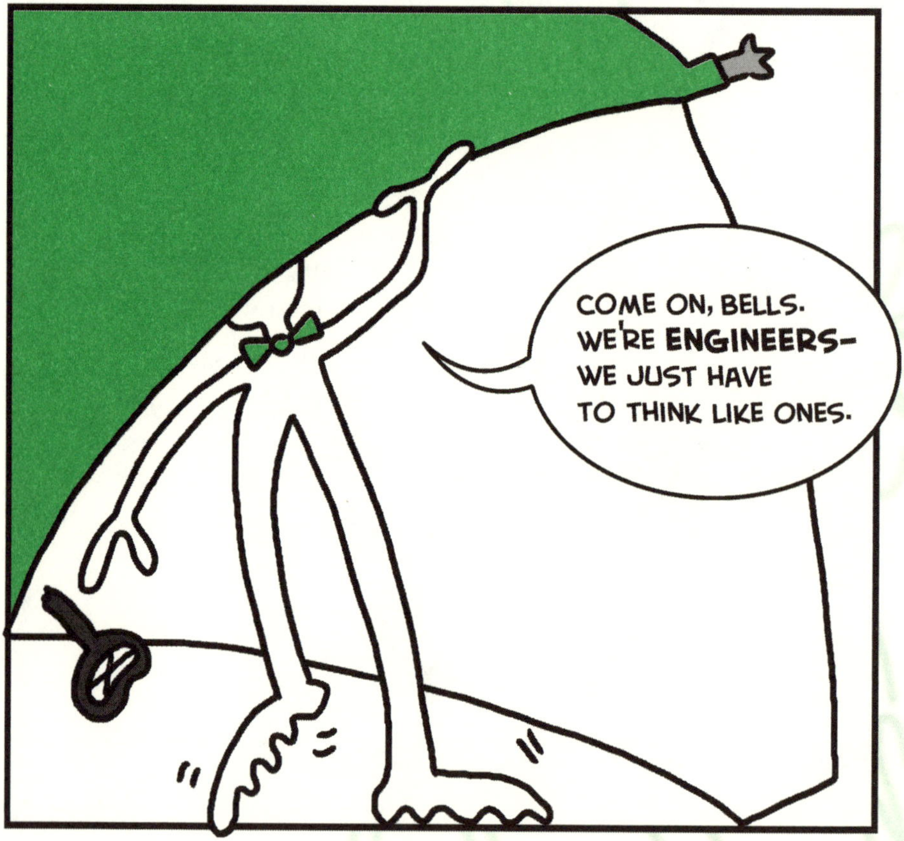
COME ON, BELLS. WE'RE **ENGINEERS**- WE JUST HAVE TO THINK LIKE ONES.

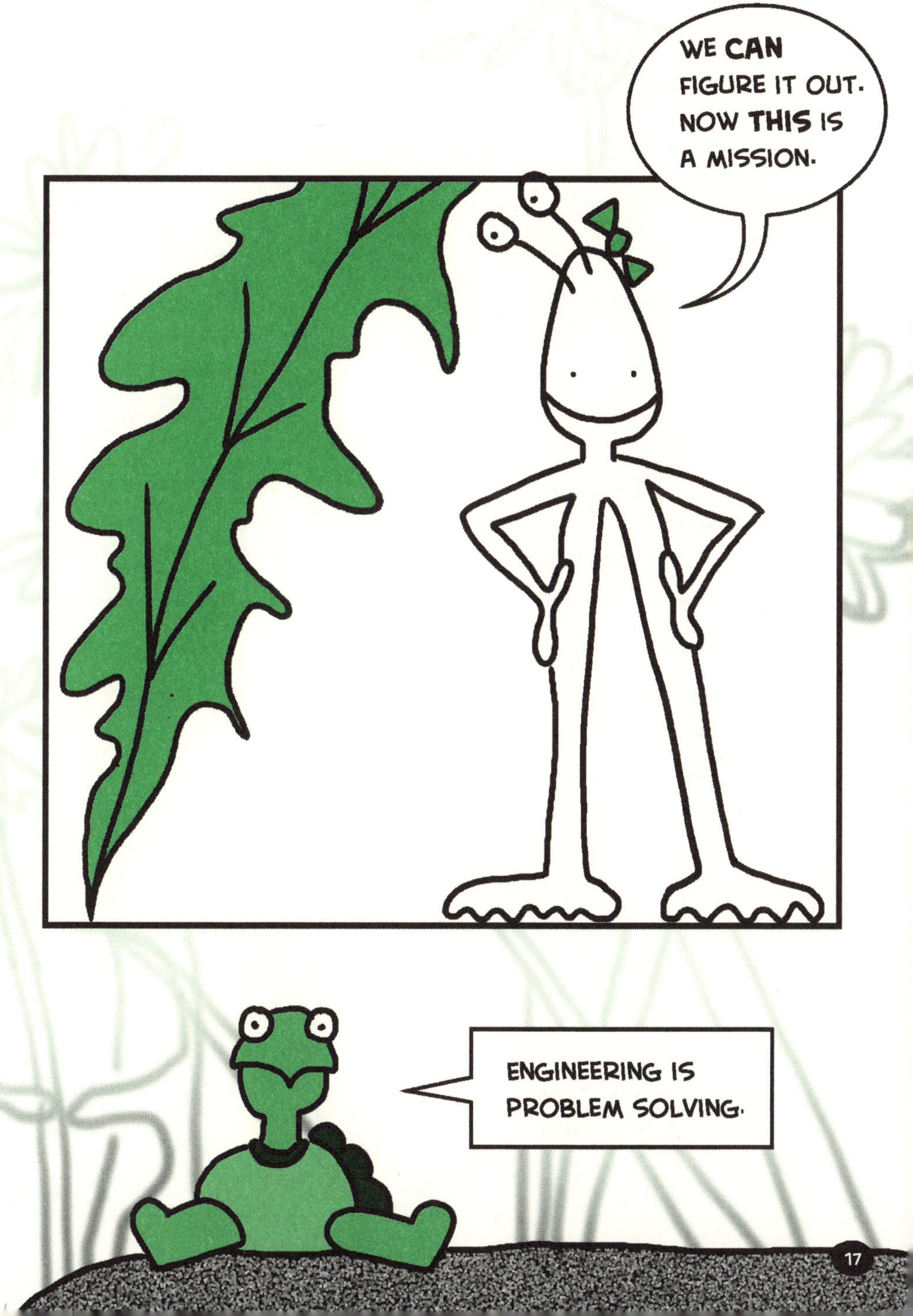
WE CAN FIGURE IT OUT. NOW THIS IS A MISSION.
ENGINEERING IS PROBLEM SOLVING.

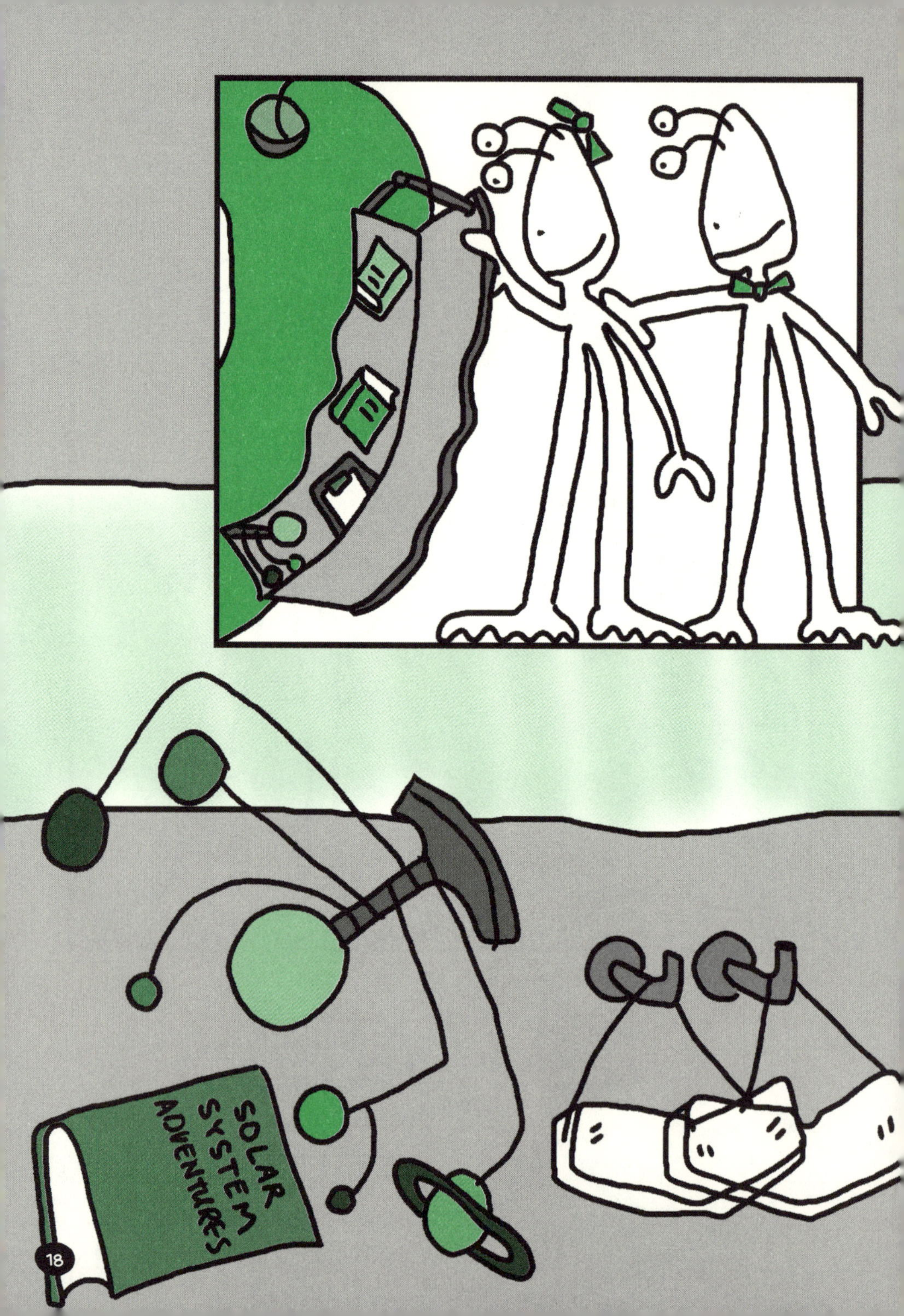
SOLAR
SYSTEM
ADVENTURES

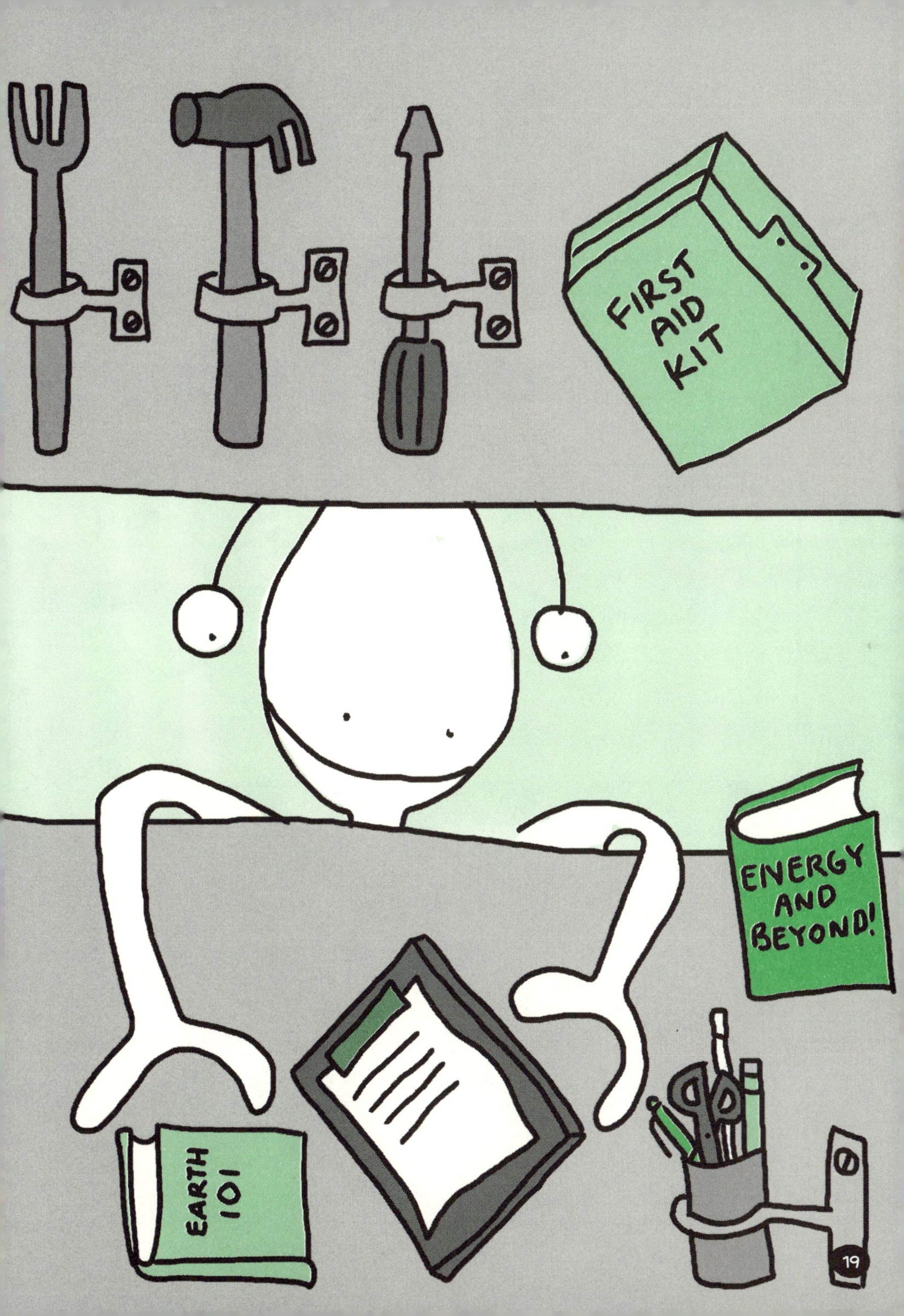
FIRST AID KIT
ENERGY AND BEYOND!
EARTH 101

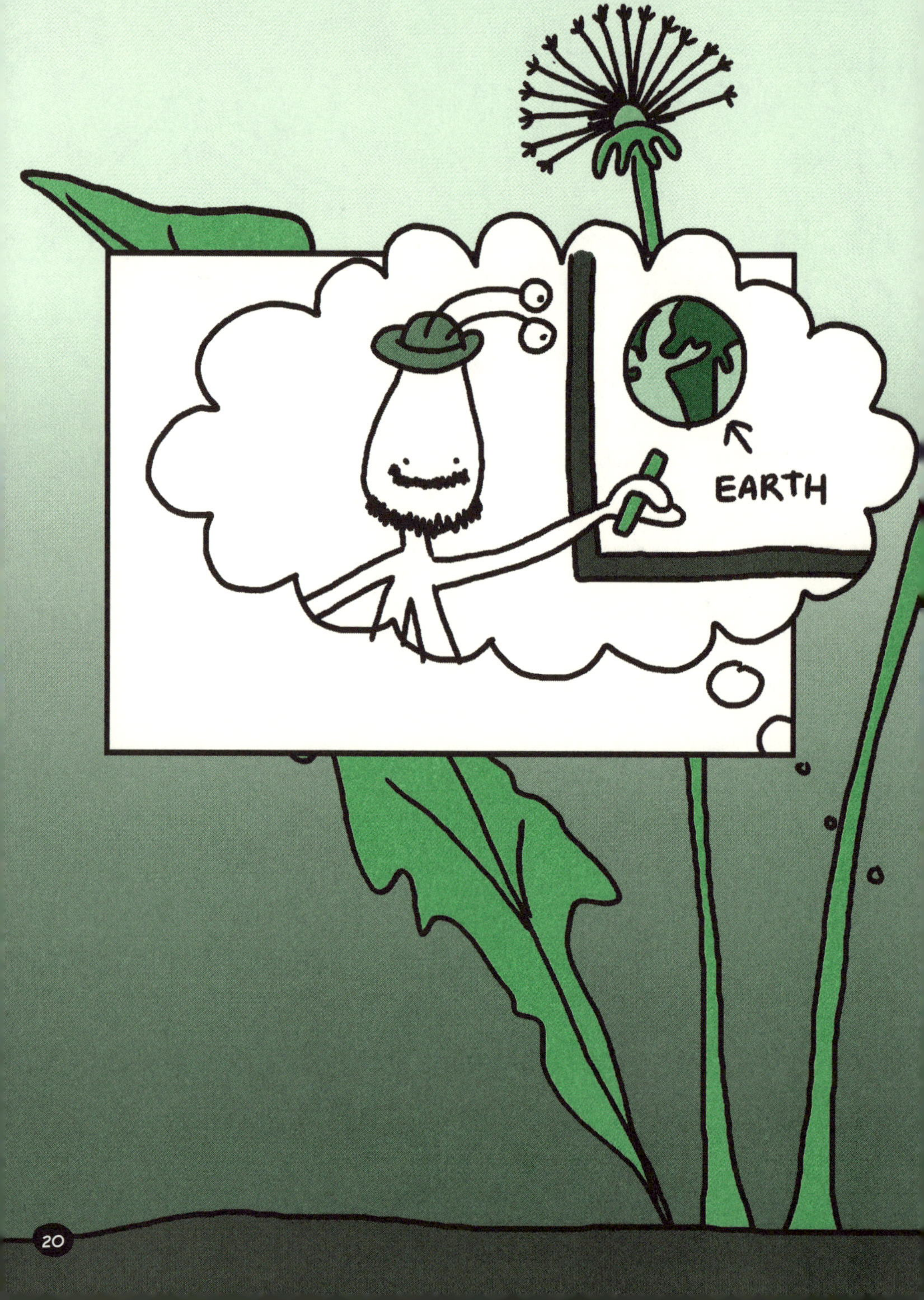
EARTH

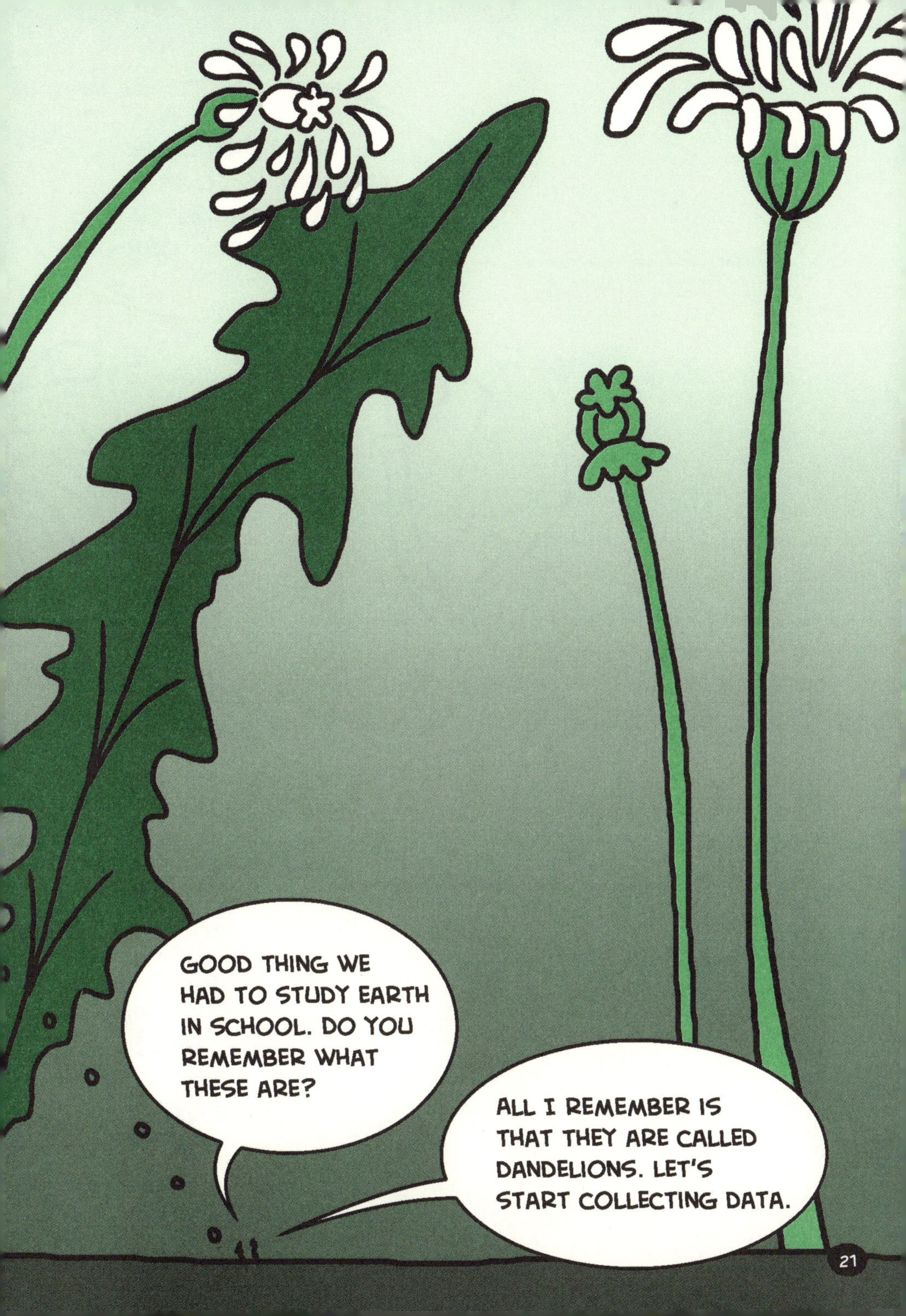
GOOD THING WE HAD TO STUDY EARTH IN SCHOOL. DO YOU REMEMBER WHAT THESE ARE?
ALL I REMEMBER IS THAT THEY ARE CALLED DANDELIONS. LET'S START COLLECTING DATA.

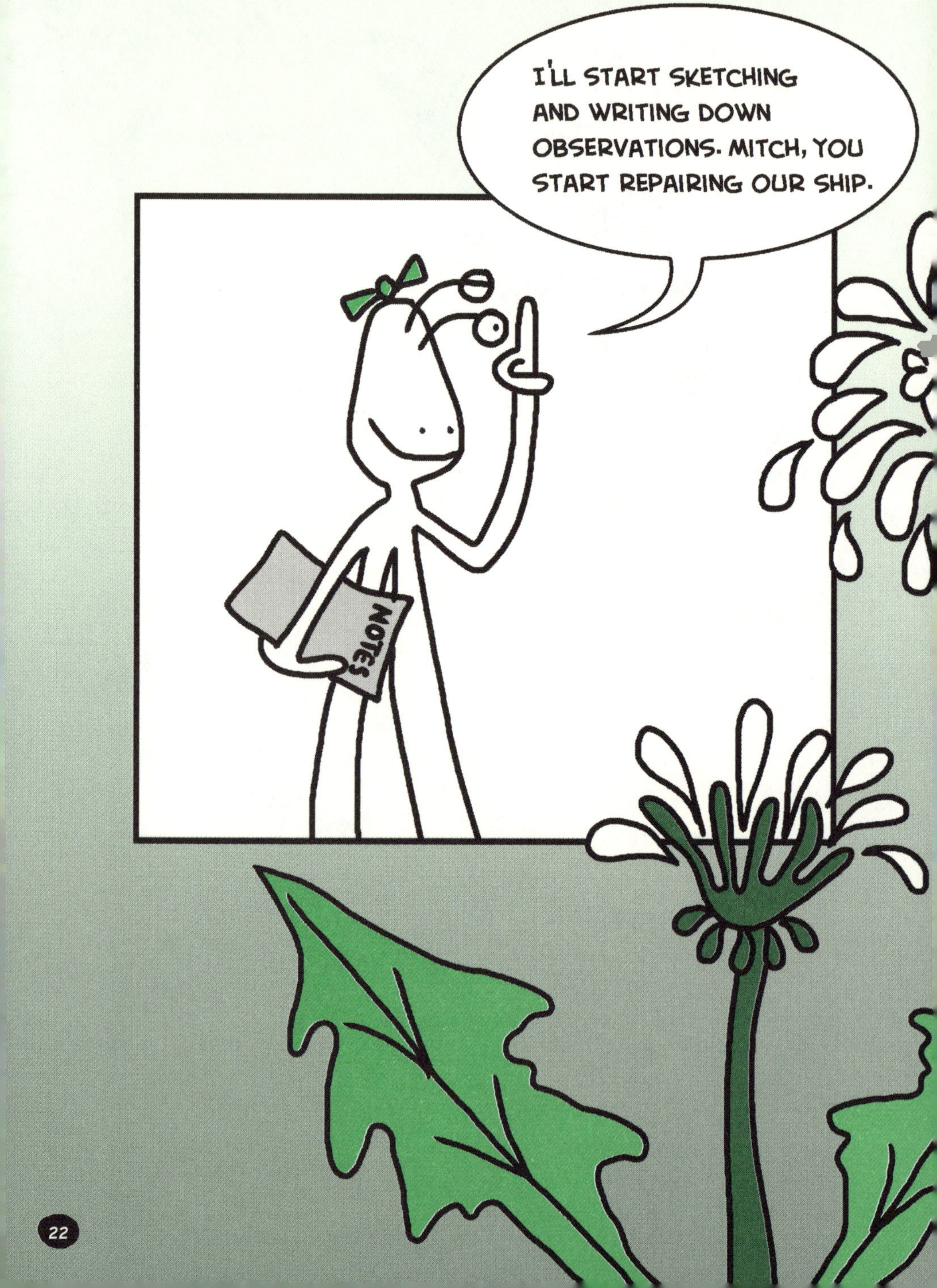
I'LL START SKETCHING AND WRITING DOWN OBSERVATIONS. MITCH, YOU START REPAIRING OUR SHIP.
NOTES

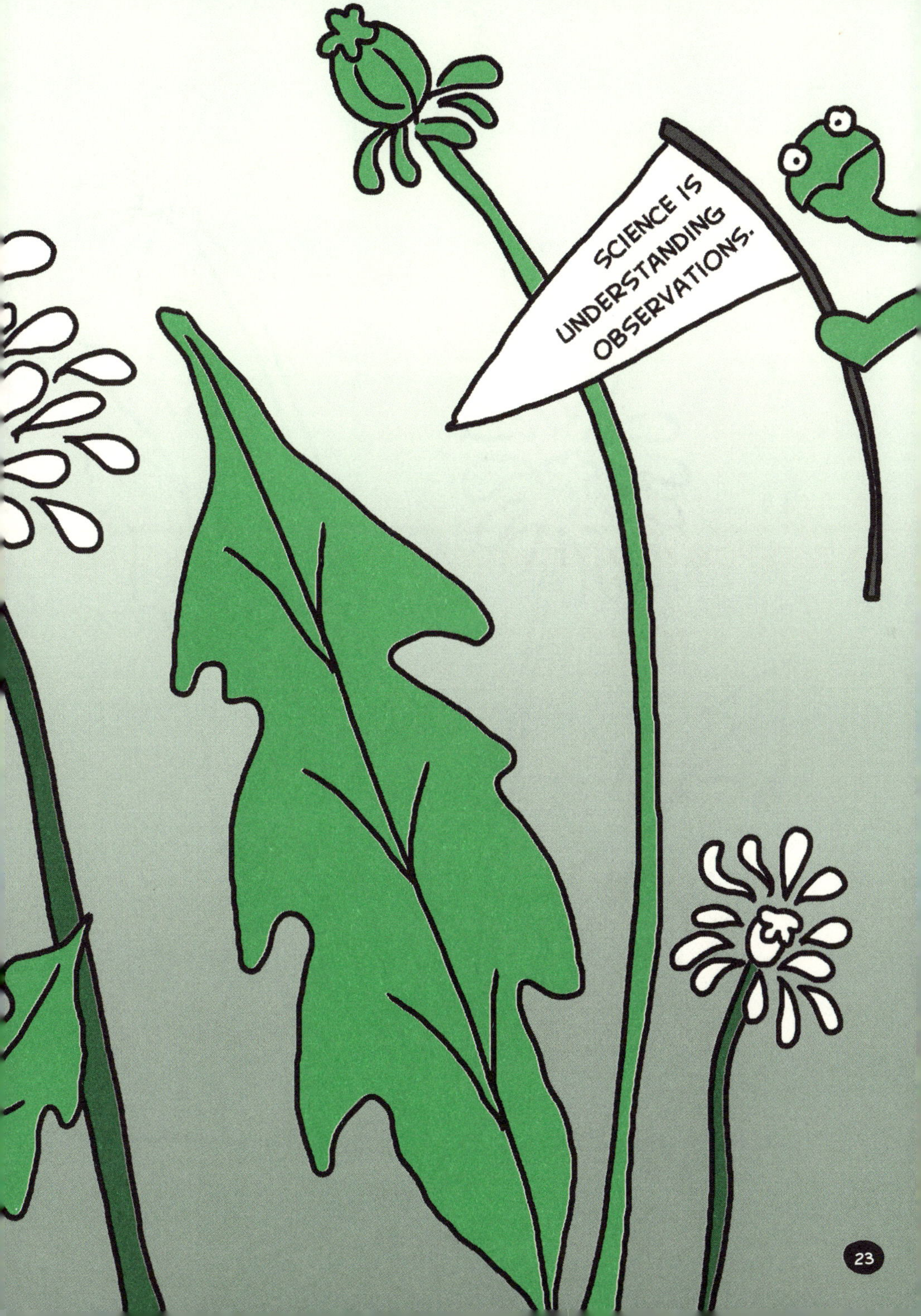
SCIENCE IS
UNDERSTANDING
OBSERVATIONS.

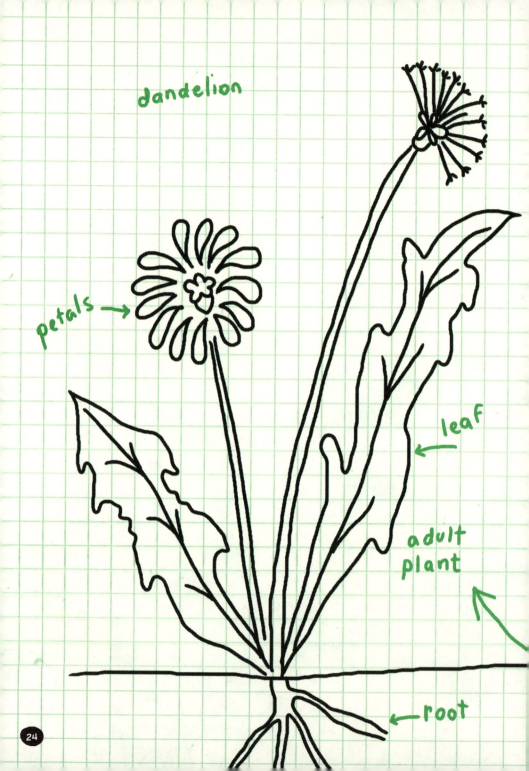

dandelion

petals →

← leaf

adult plant

← root

24

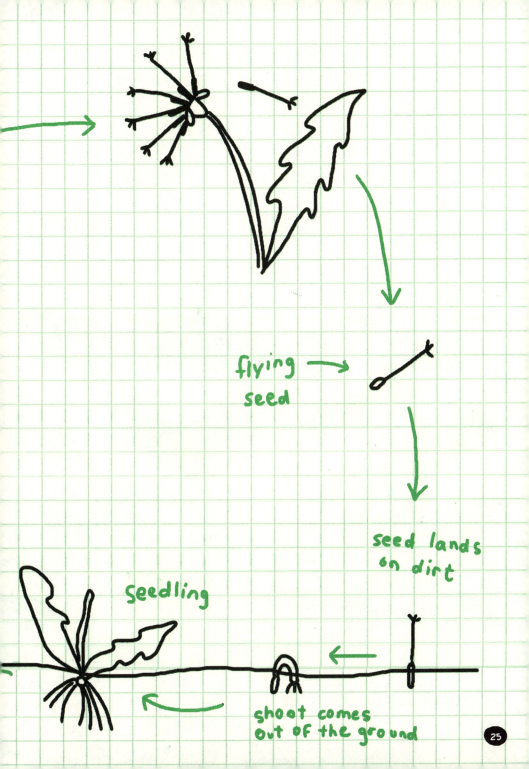

flying → seed

seed lands on dirt

Seedling

shoot comes out of the ground

25

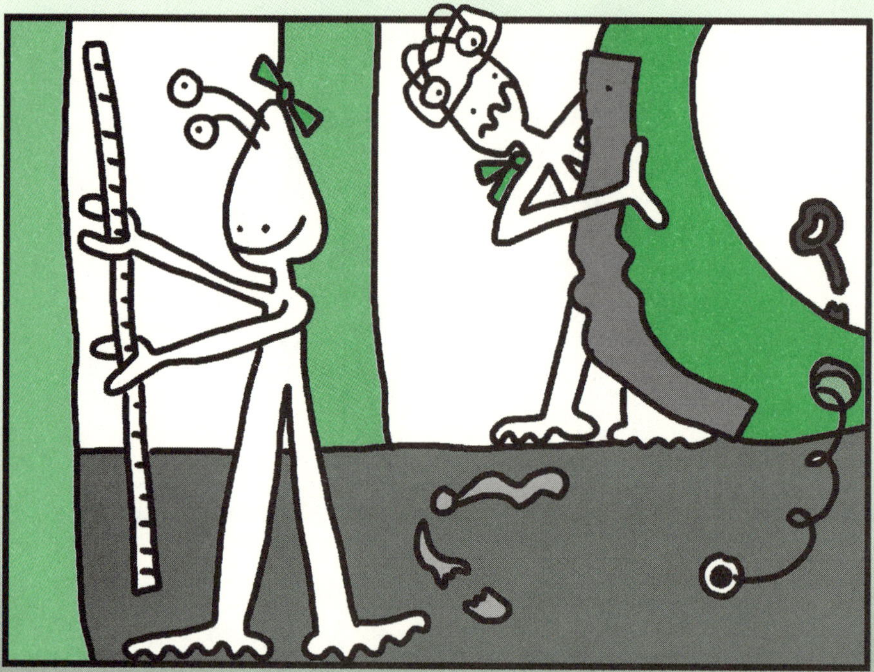

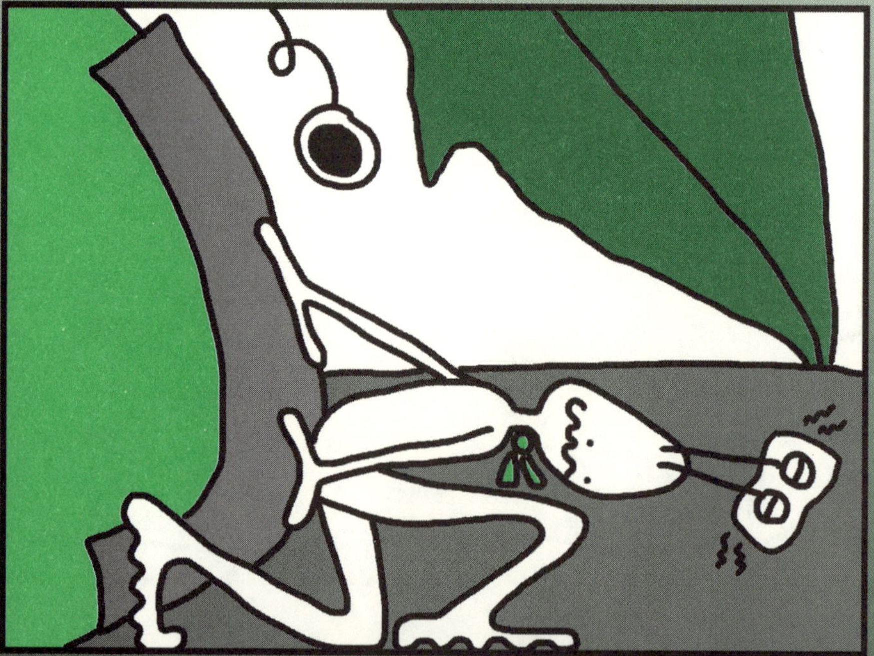

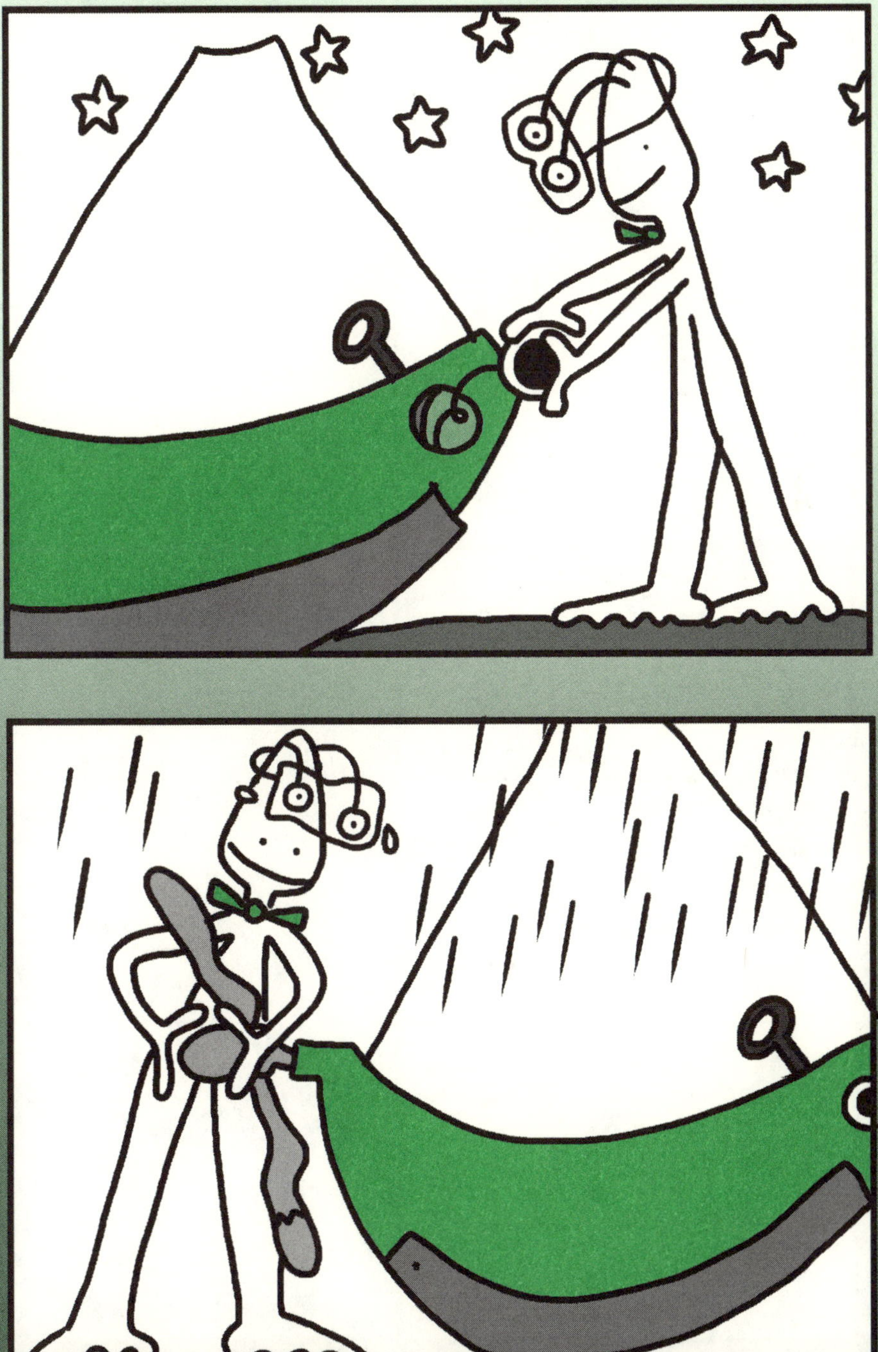

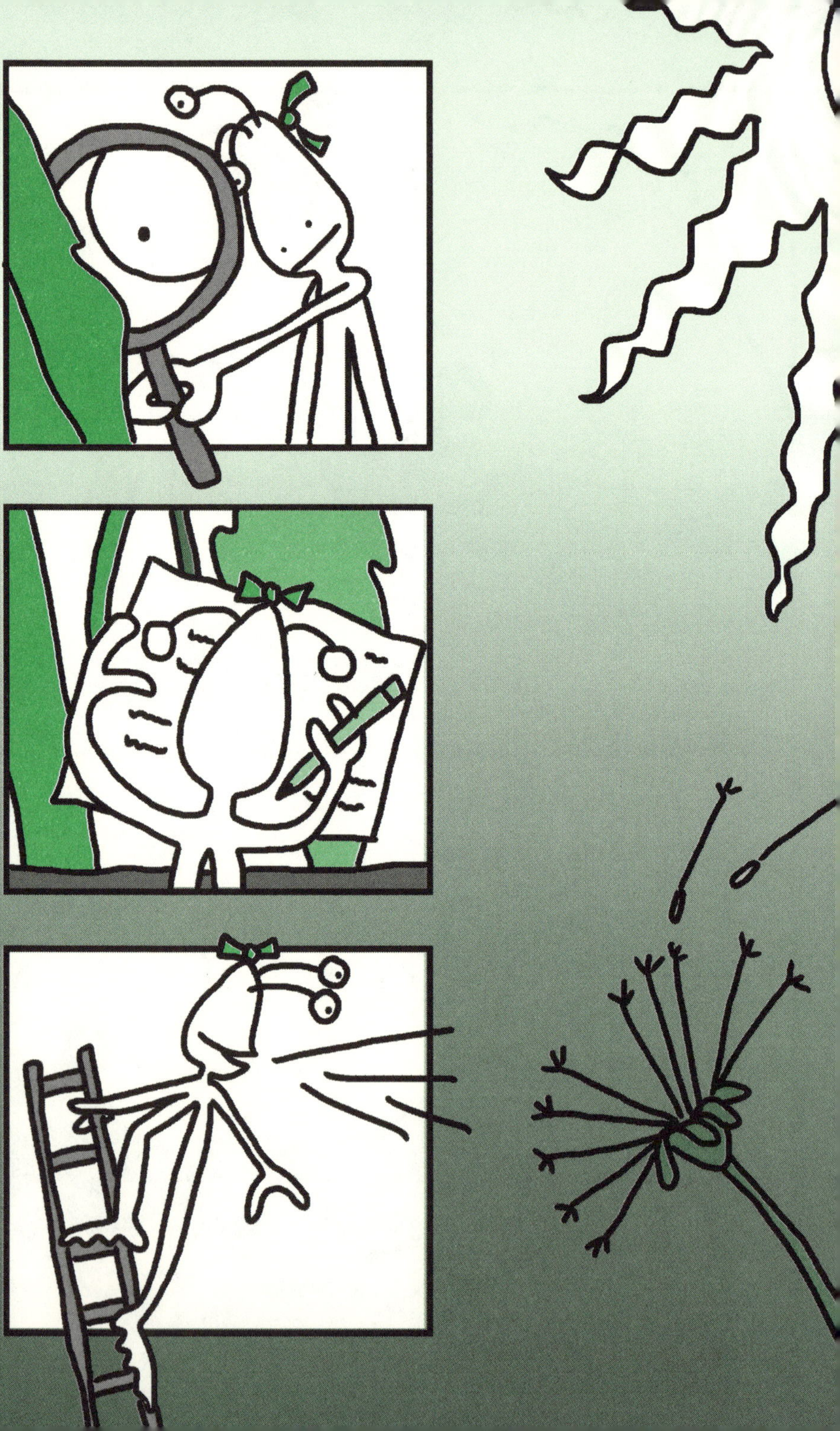

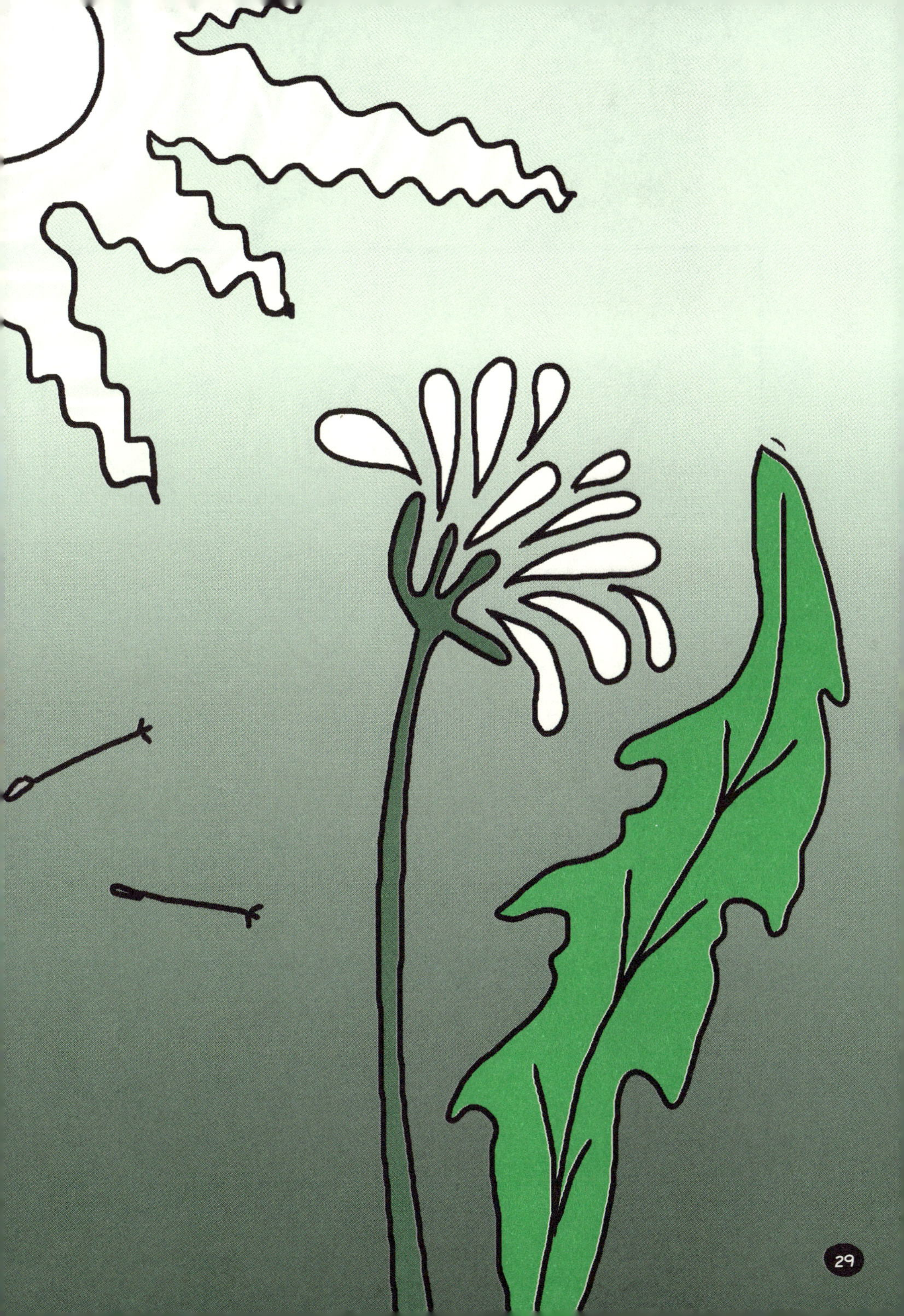

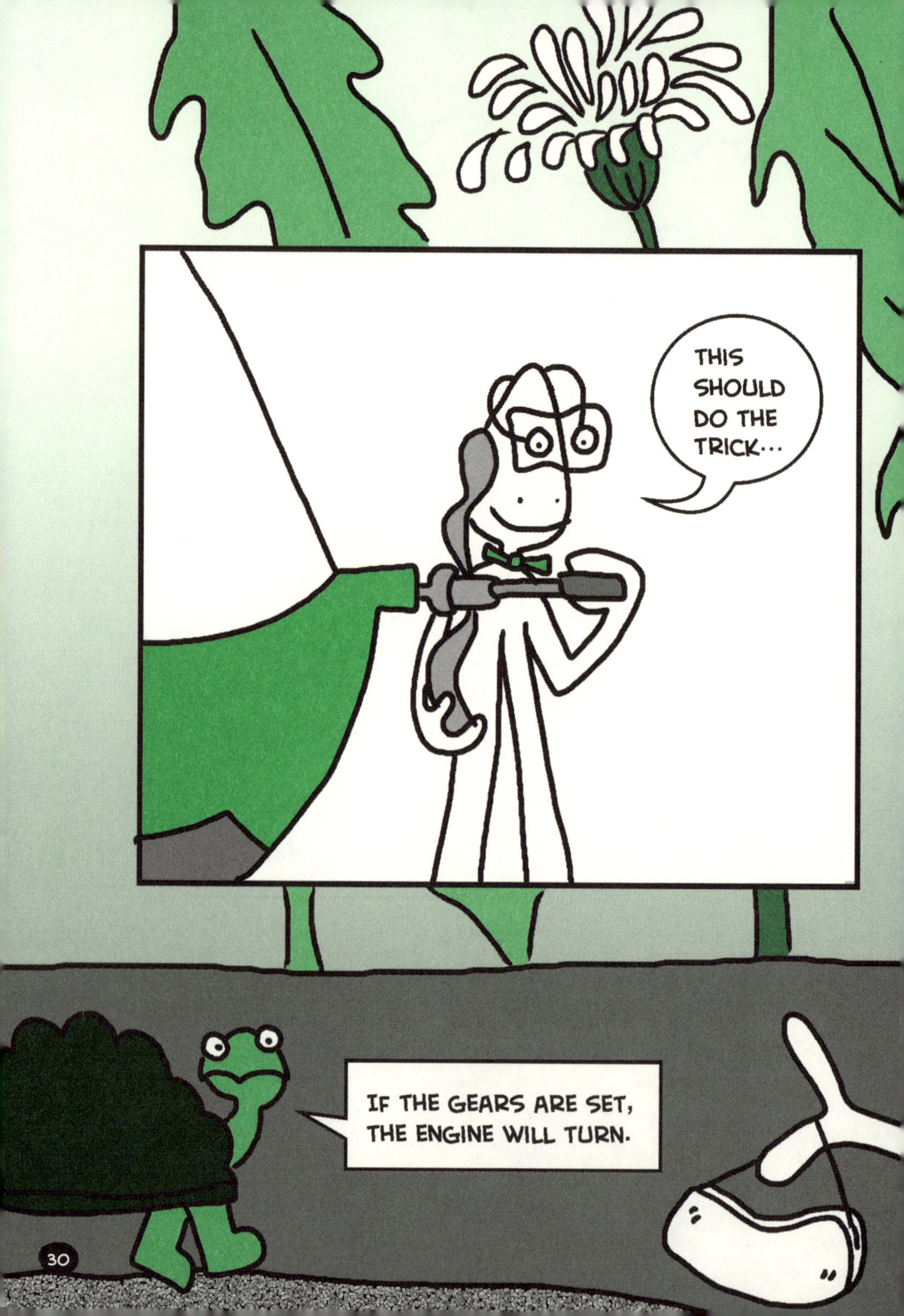
THIS SHOULD DO THE TRICK...
IF THE GEARS ARE SET, THE ENGINE WILL TURN.

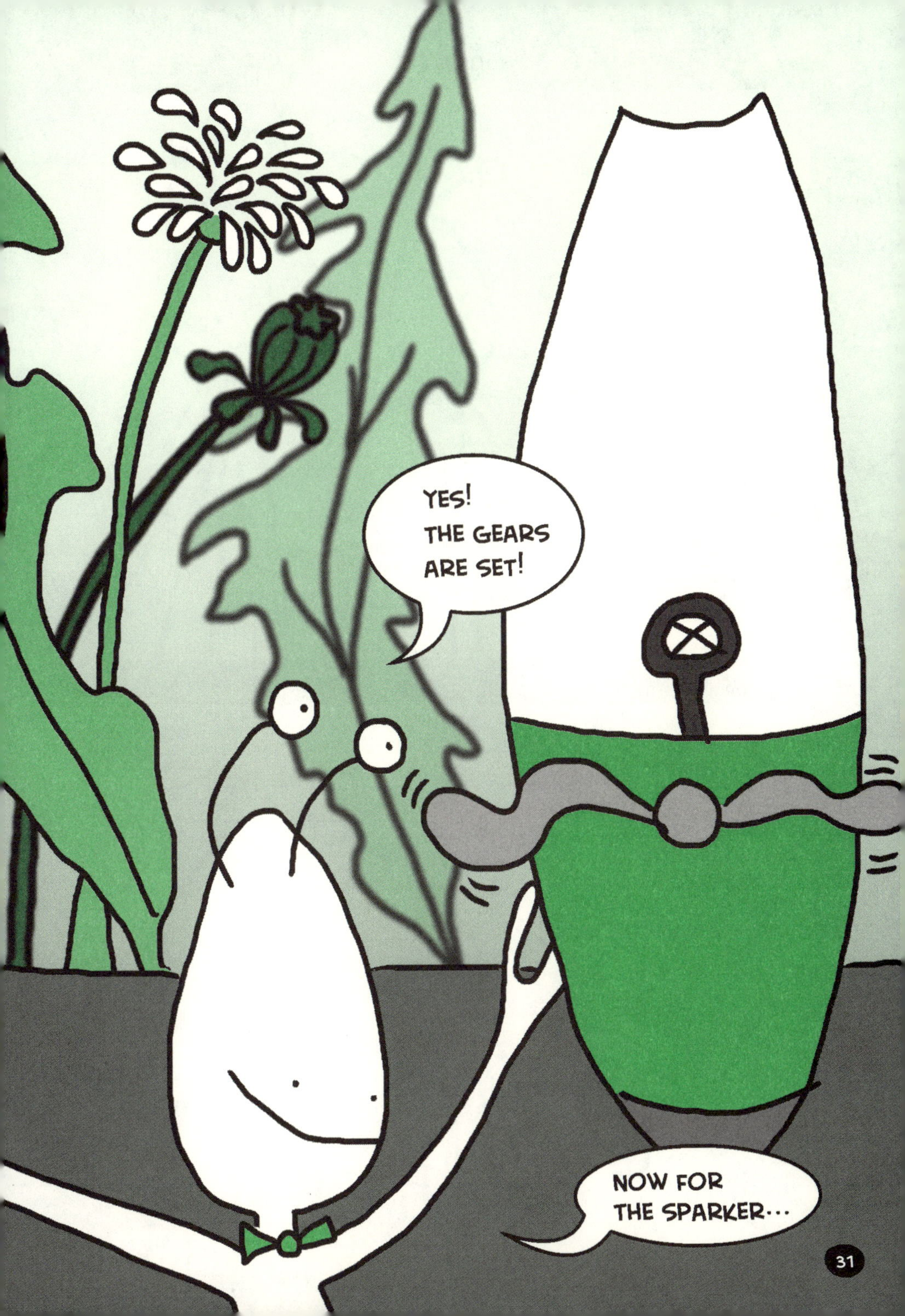
YES! THE GEARS ARE SET!
NOW FOR THE SPARKER...

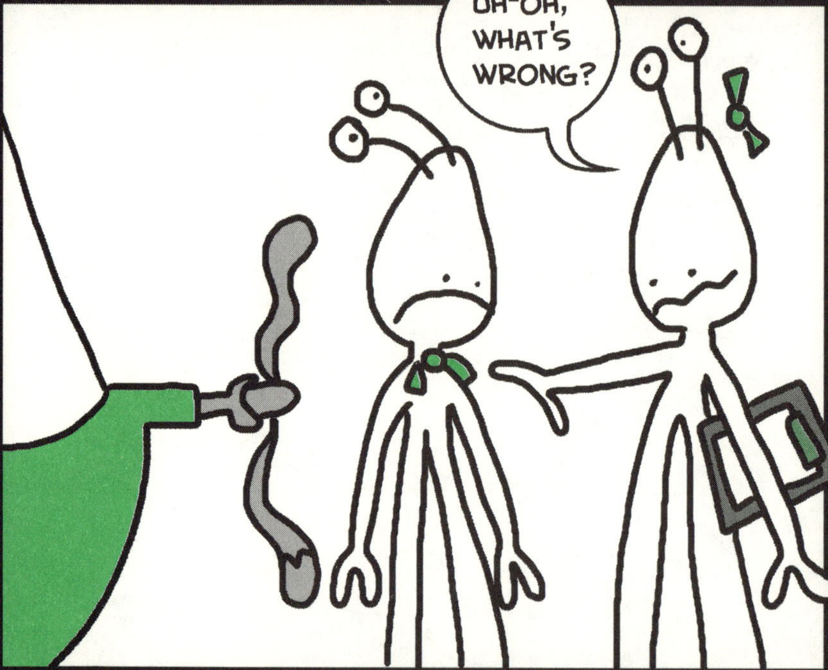

UH-OH, WHAT'S WRONG?

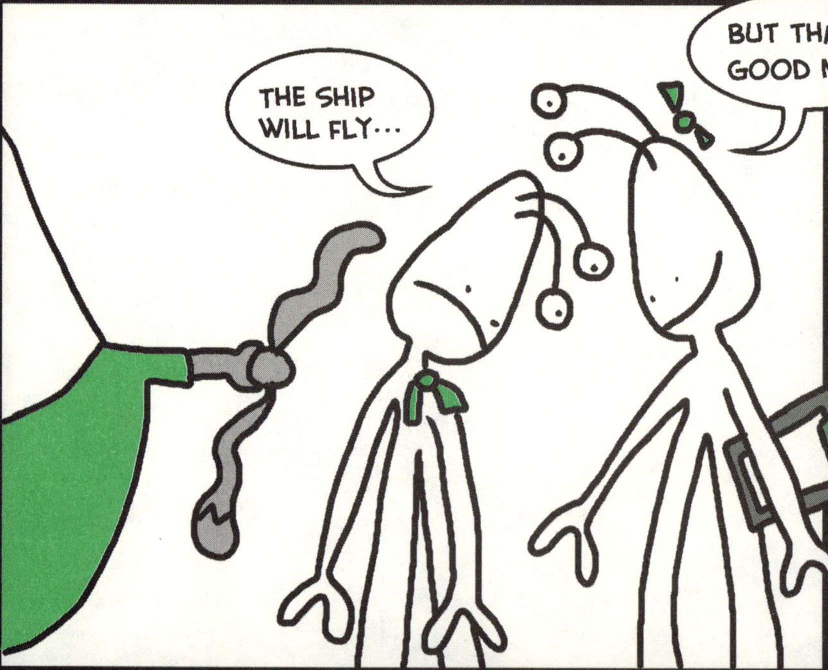

THE SHIP WILL FLY...
BUT THAT'S GOOD NEWS.

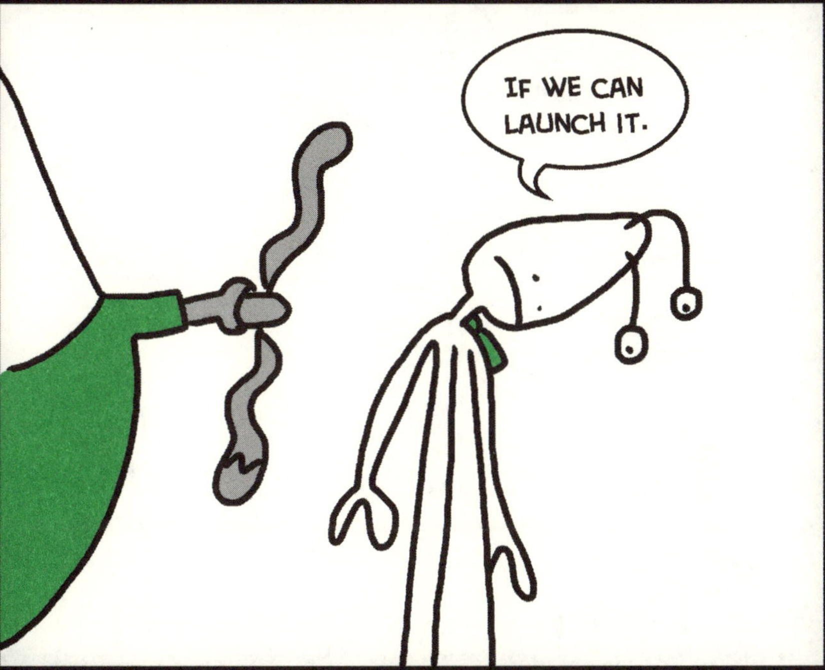
IF WE CAN LAUNCH IT.

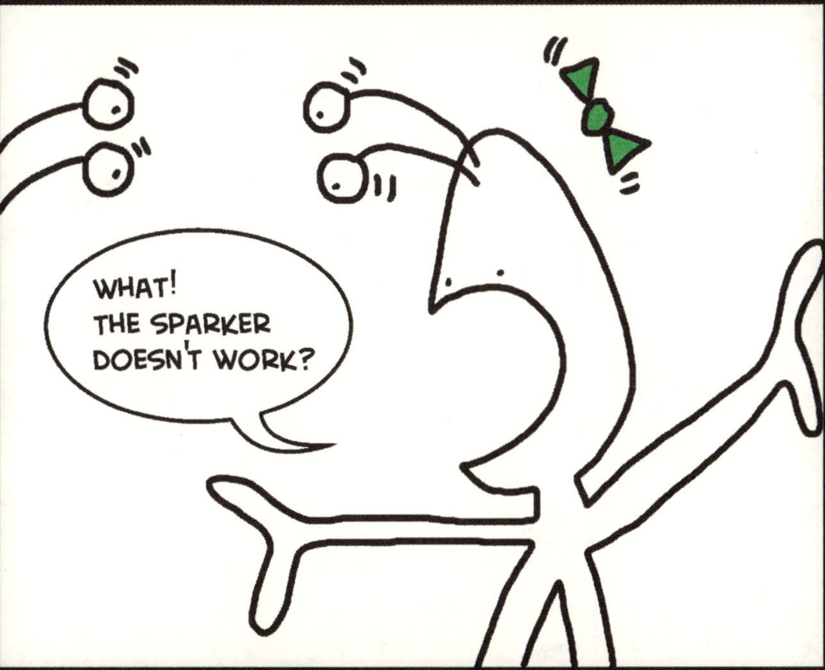
WHAT!
THE SPARKER DOESN'T WORK?

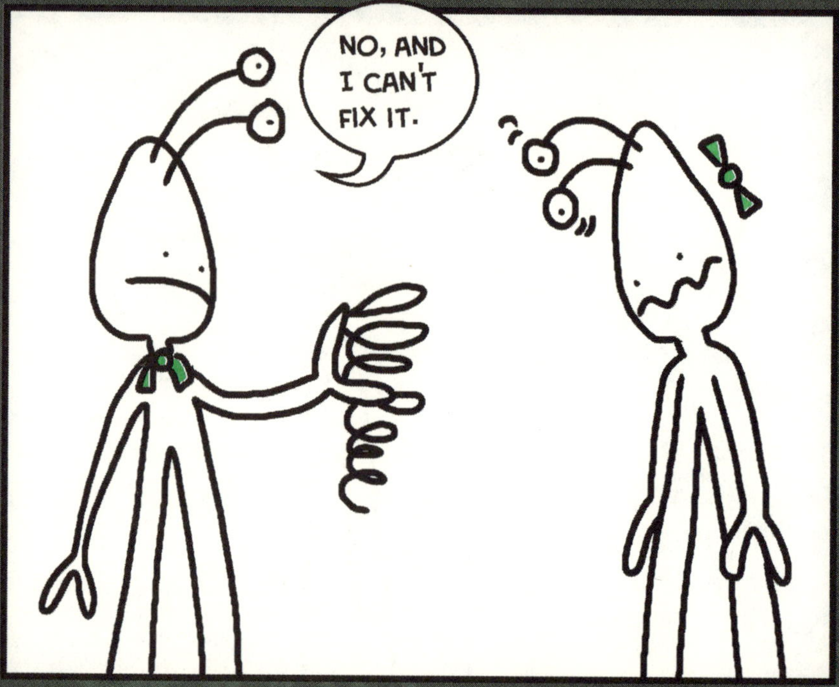
NO, AND I CAN'T FIX IT.

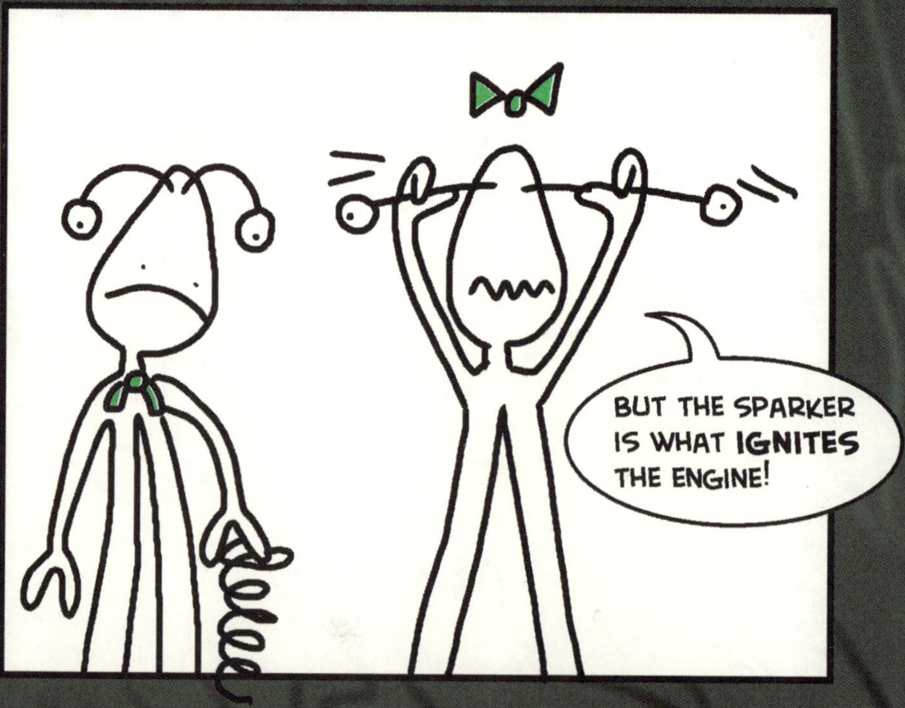
BUT THE SPARKER IS WHAT IGNITES THE ENGINE!

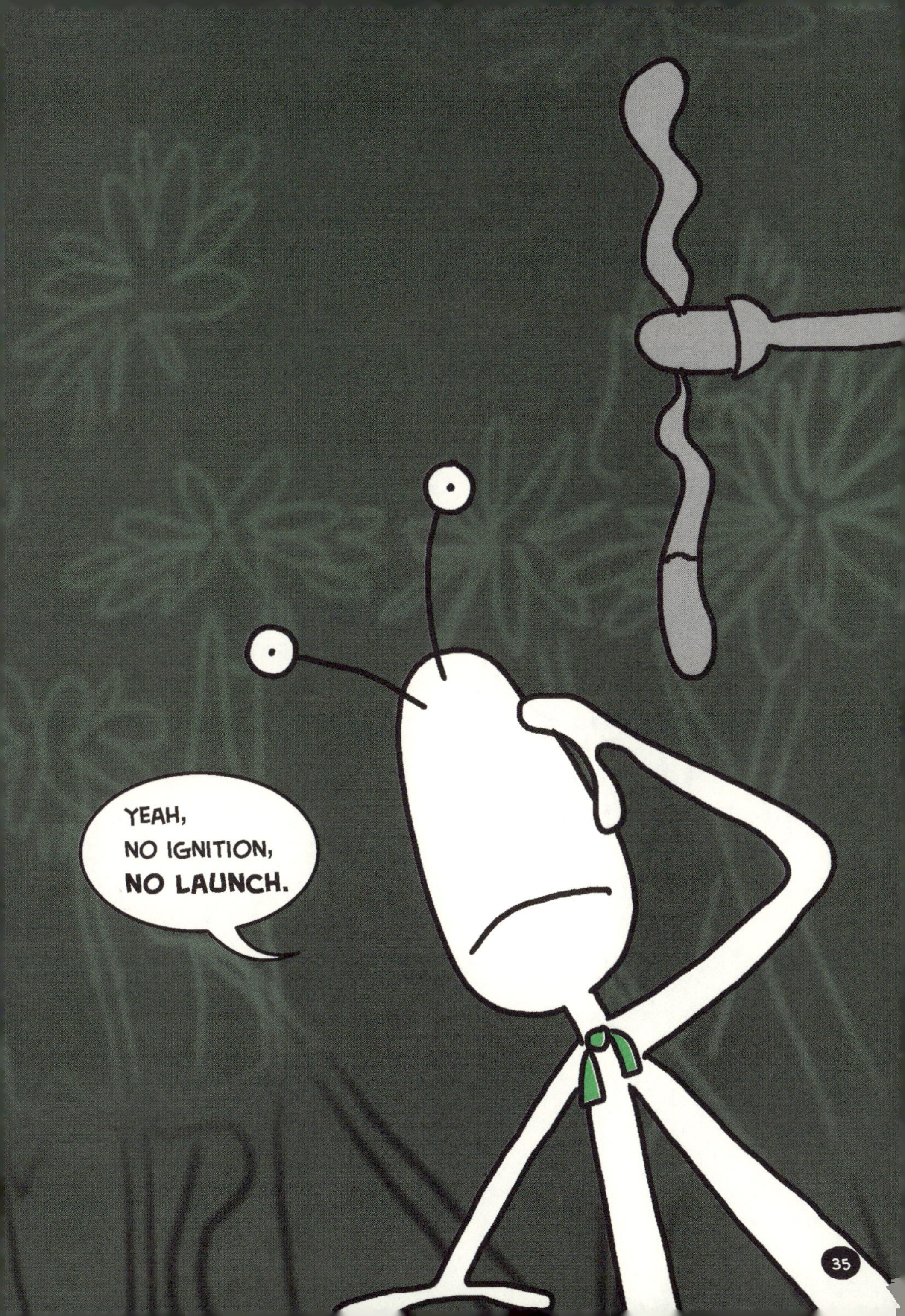
YEAH,
NO IGNITION,
NO LAUNCH.

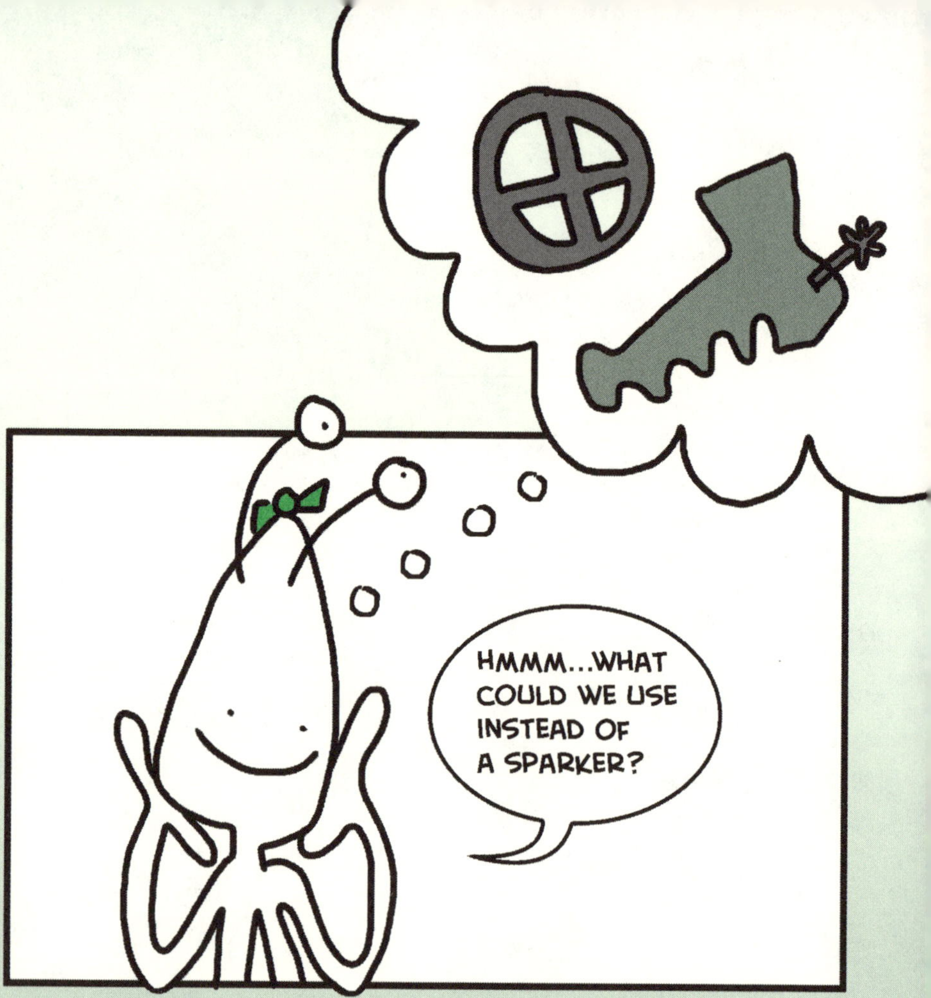
HMMM...WHAT COULD WE USE INSTEAD OF A SPARKER?

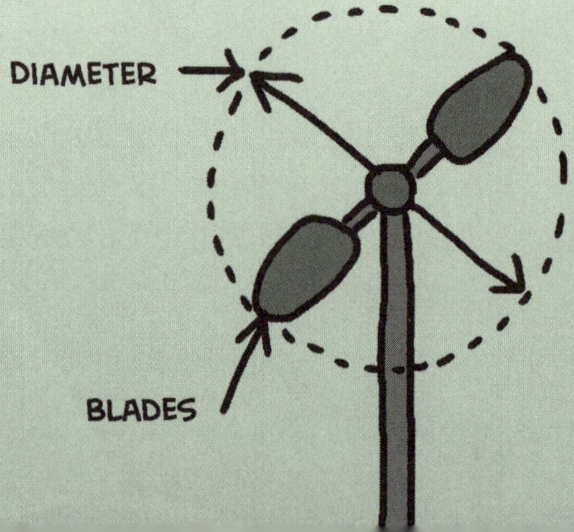
DIAMETER
BLADES

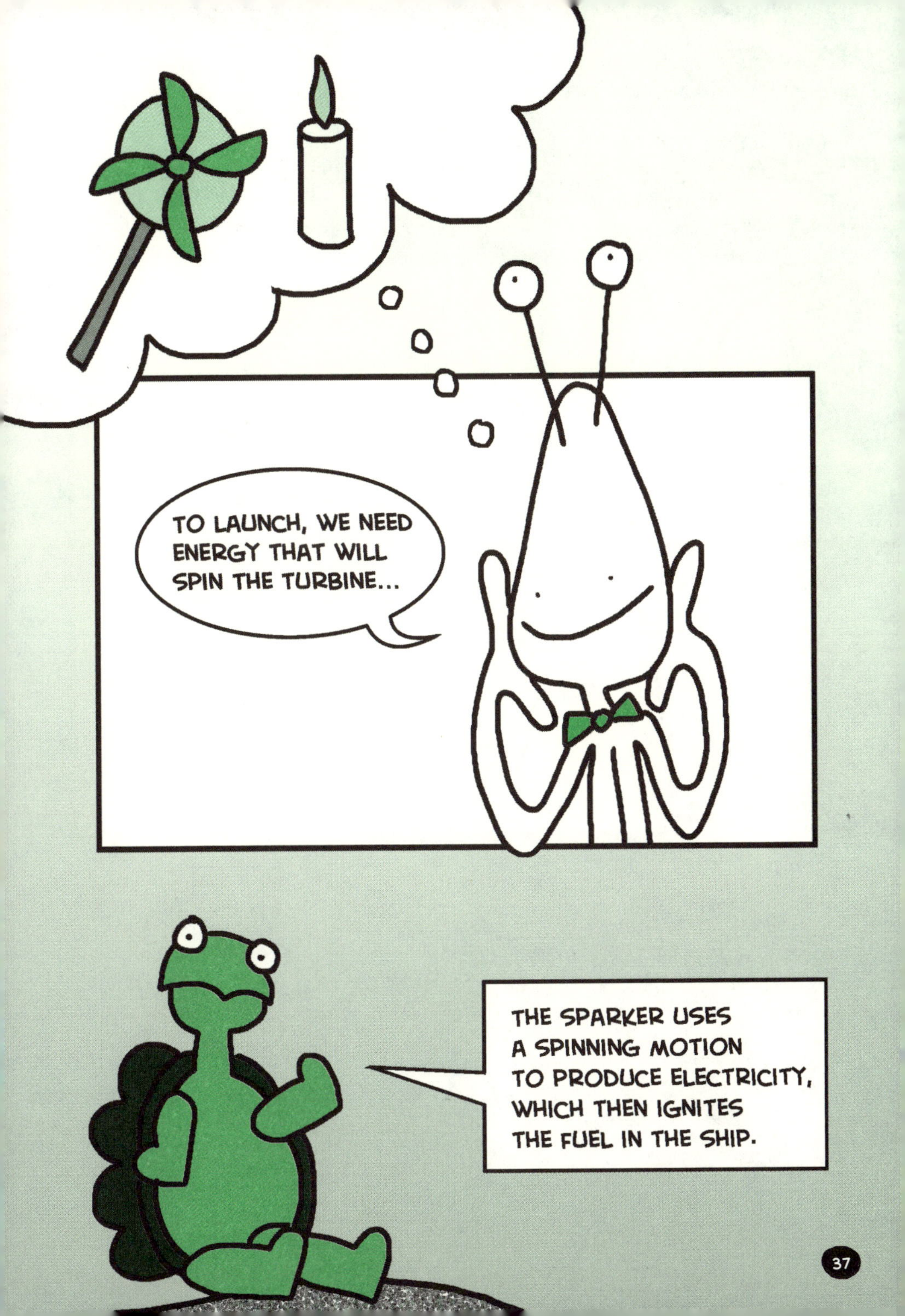
TO LAUNCH, WE NEED ENERGY THAT WILL SPIN THE TURBINE...
THE SPARKER USES A SPINNING MOTION TO PRODUCE ELECTRICITY, WHICH THEN IGNITES THE FUEL IN THE SHIP.

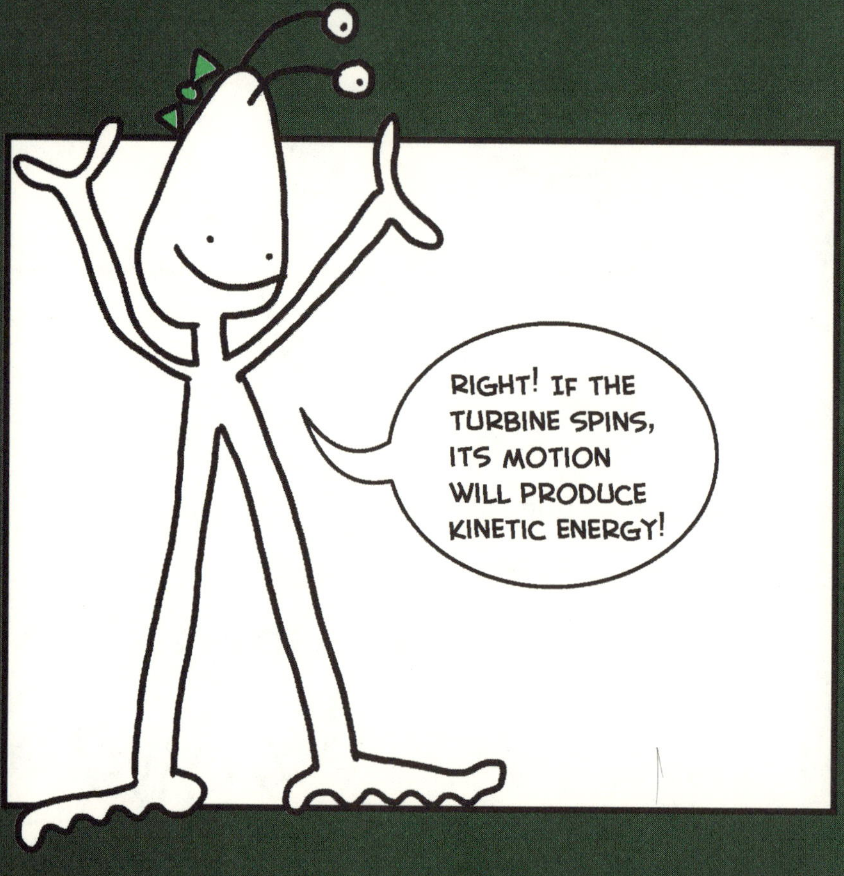
RIGHT! IF THE TURBINE SPINS, ITS MOTION WILL PRODUCE KINETIC ENERGY!

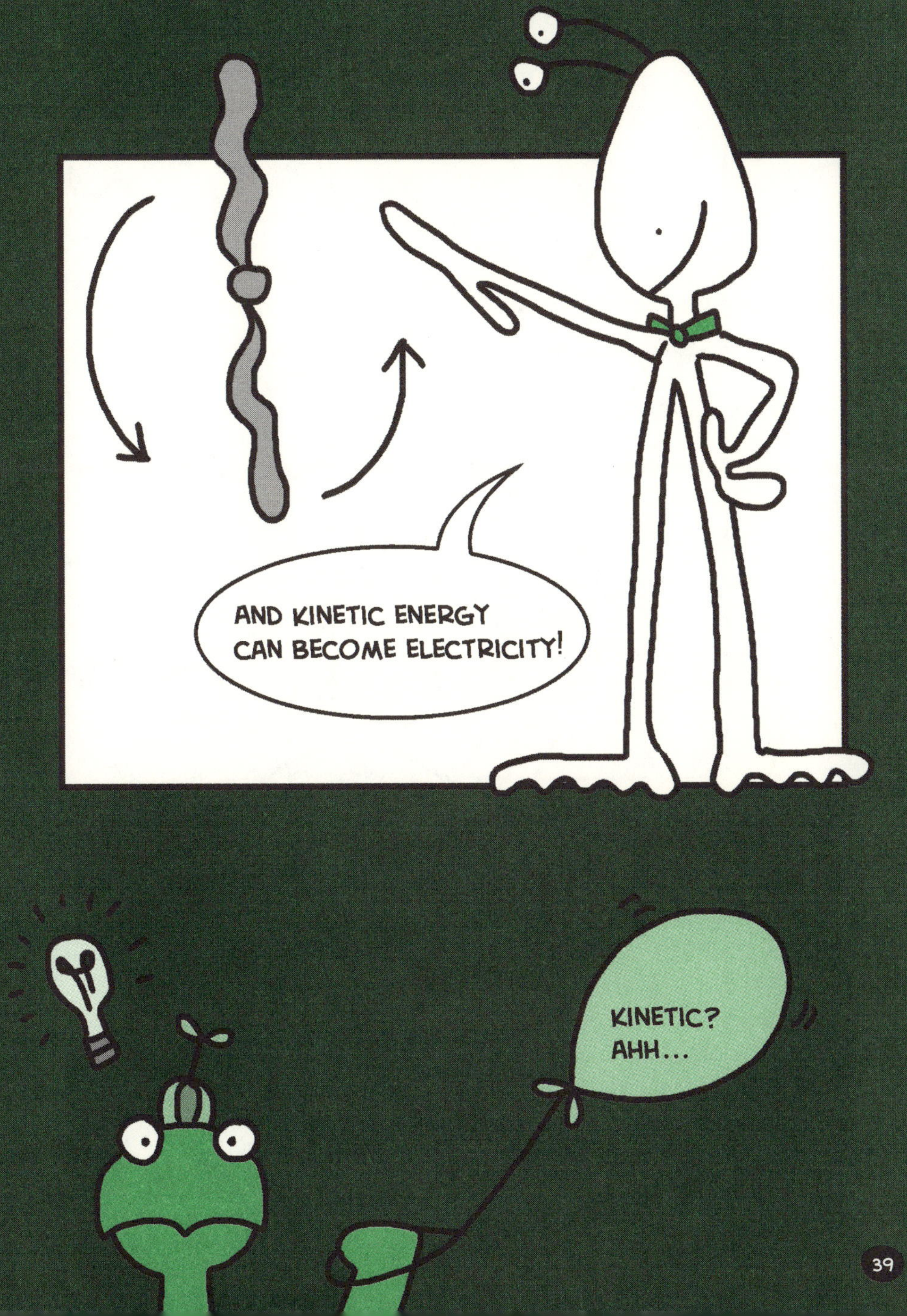
AND KINETIC ENERGY CAN BECOME ELECTRICITY!
KINETIC? AHH...

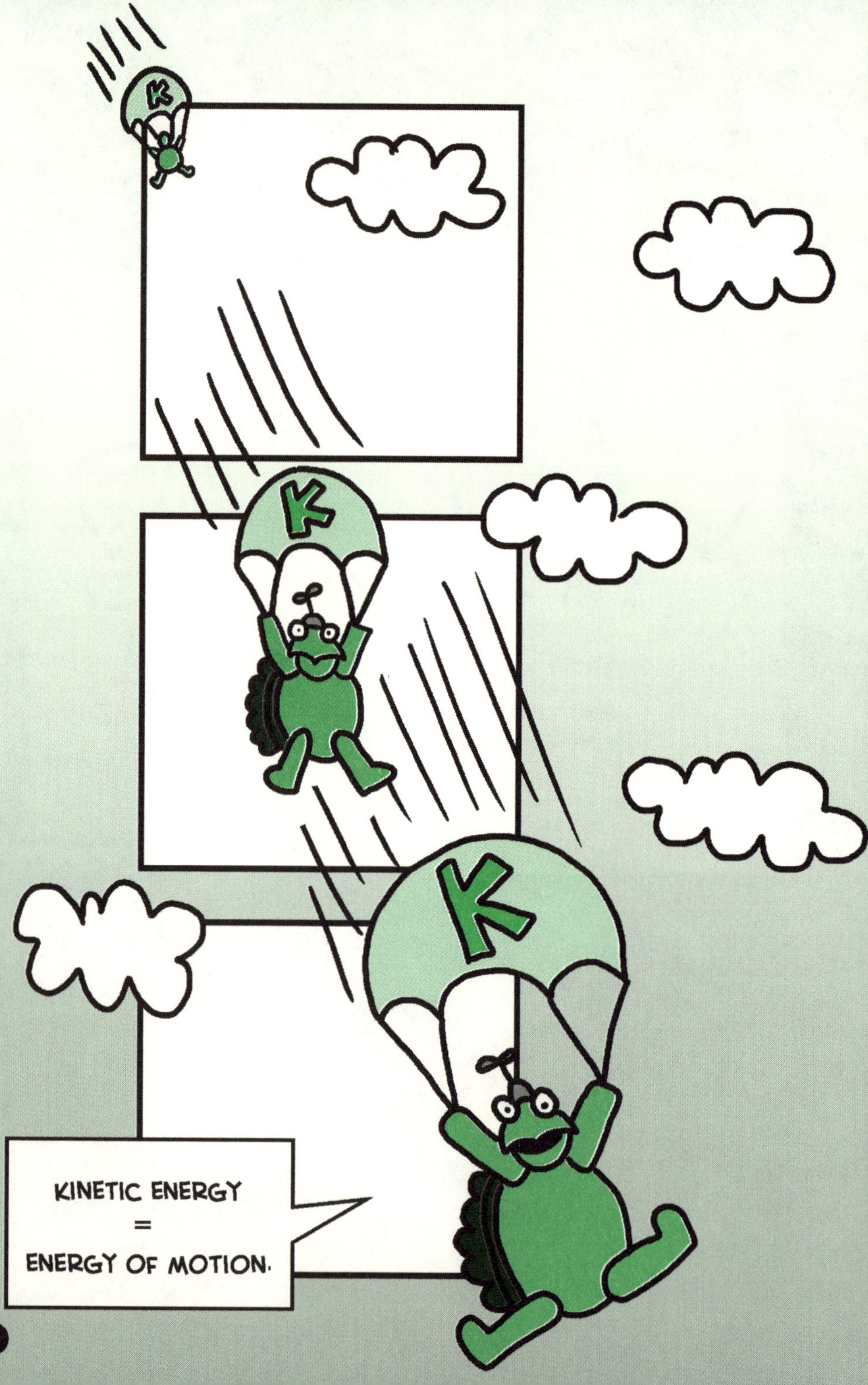
KINETIC ENERGY
=
ENERGY OF MOTION.

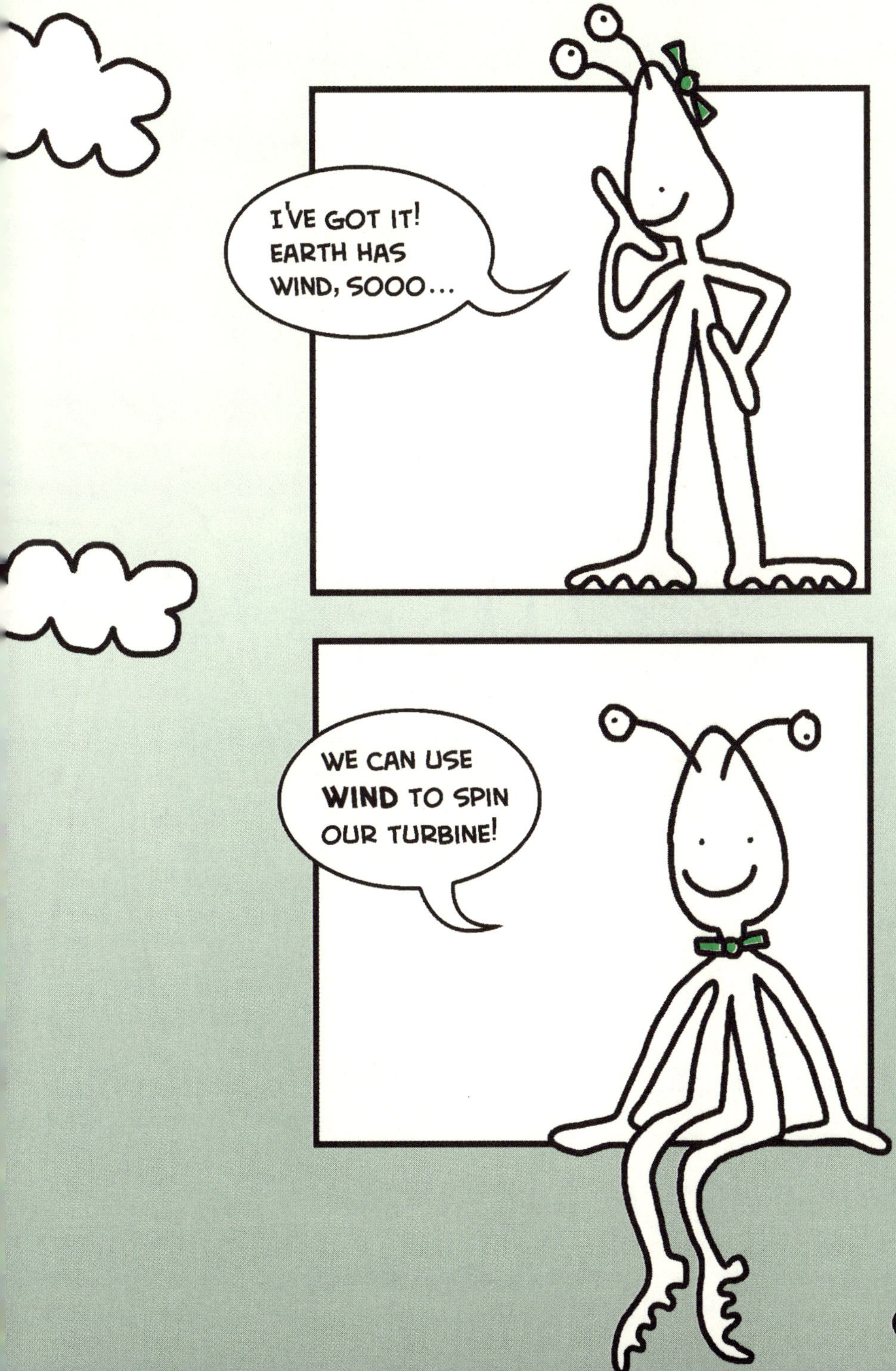
I'VE GOT IT! EARTH HAS WIND, SOOO...
WE CAN USE **WIND** TO SPIN OUR TURBINE!

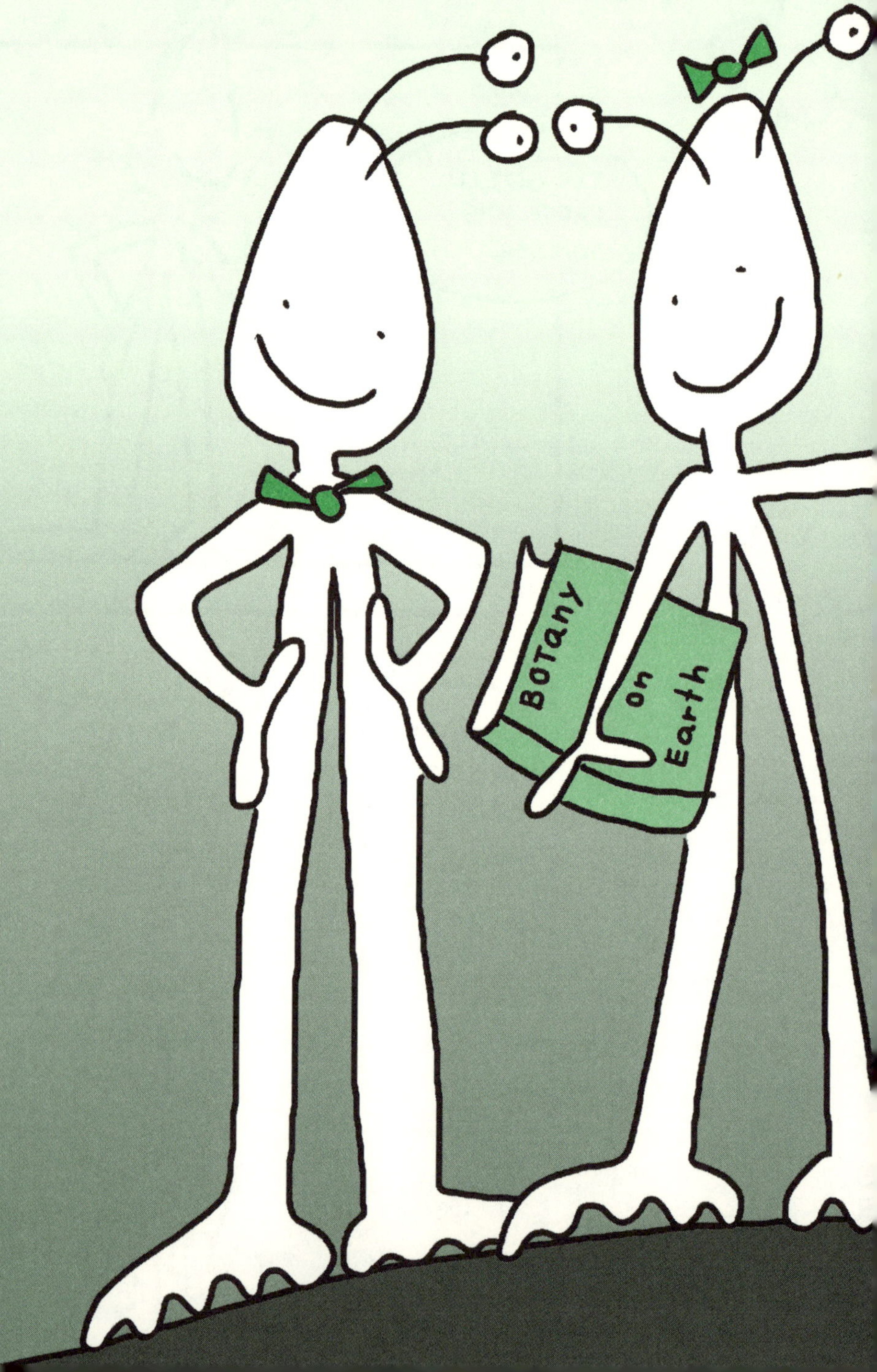
BOTany
on
Earth

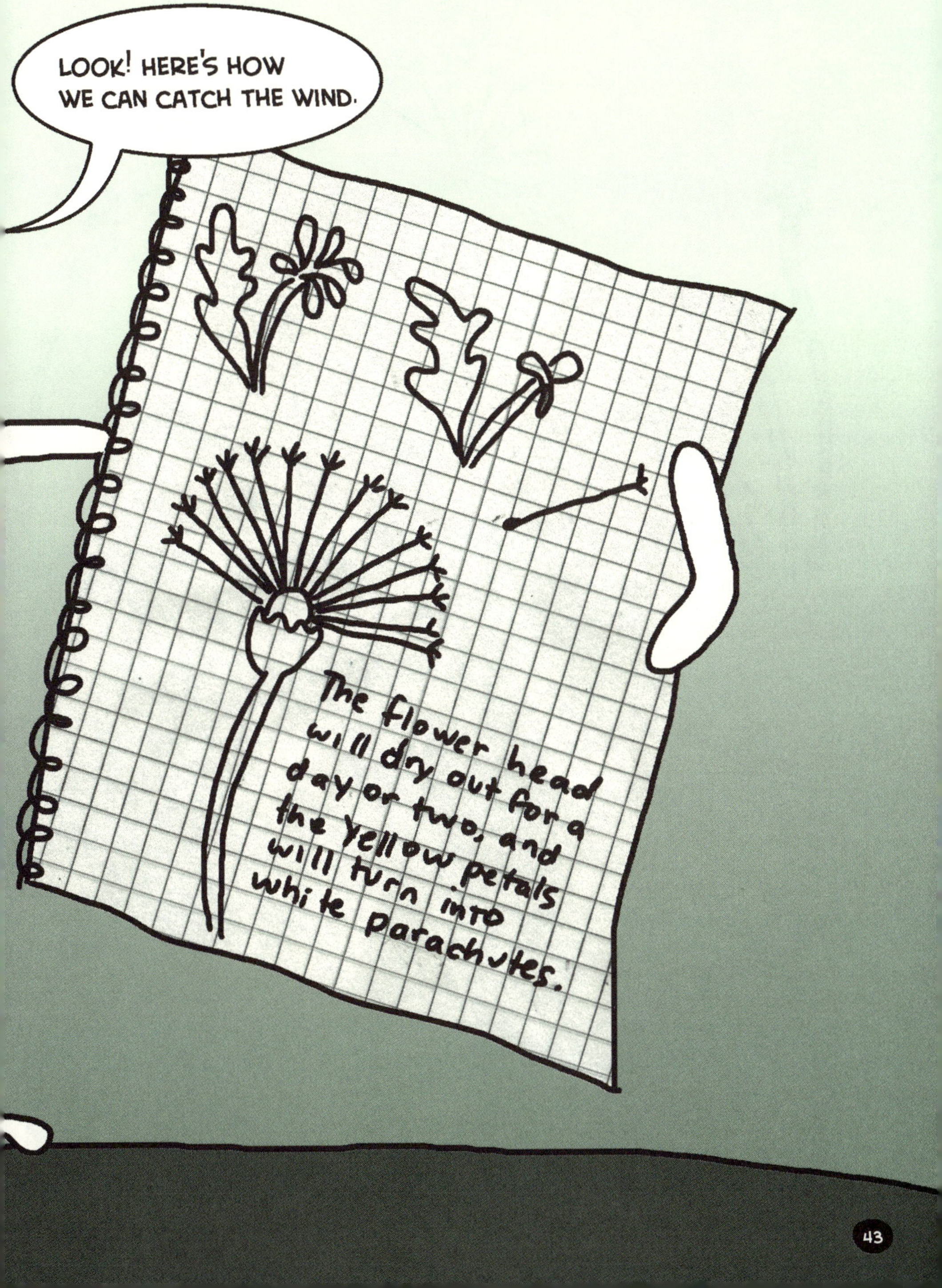
LOOK! HERE'S HOW WE CAN CATCH THE WIND.
The flower head will dry out for a day or two, and the yellow petals will turn into white parachutes.

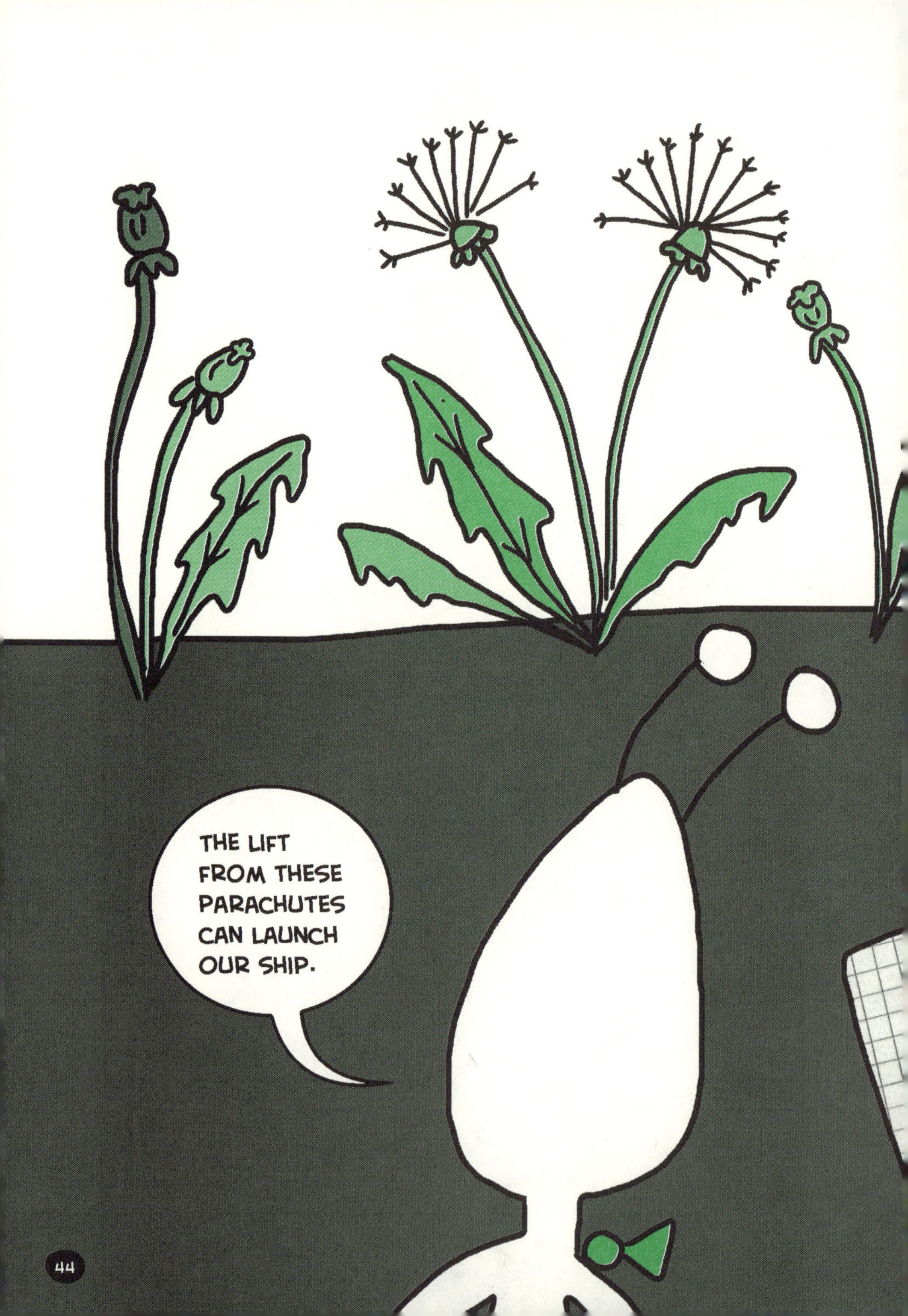
THE LIFT FROM THESE PARACHUTES CAN LAUNCH OUR SHIP.

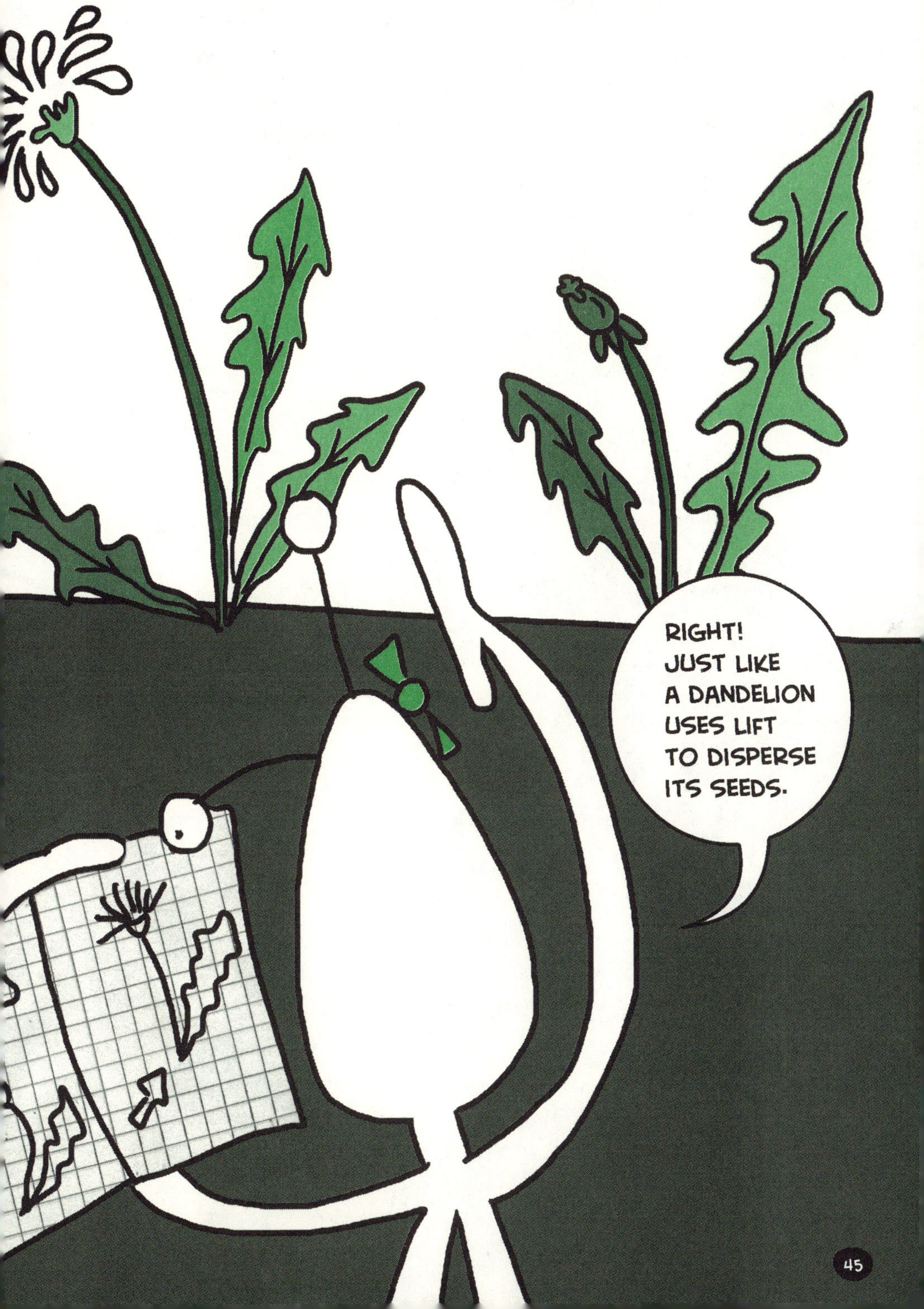
RIGHT!
JUST LIKE
A DANDELION
USES LIFT
TO DISPERSE
ITS SEEDS.

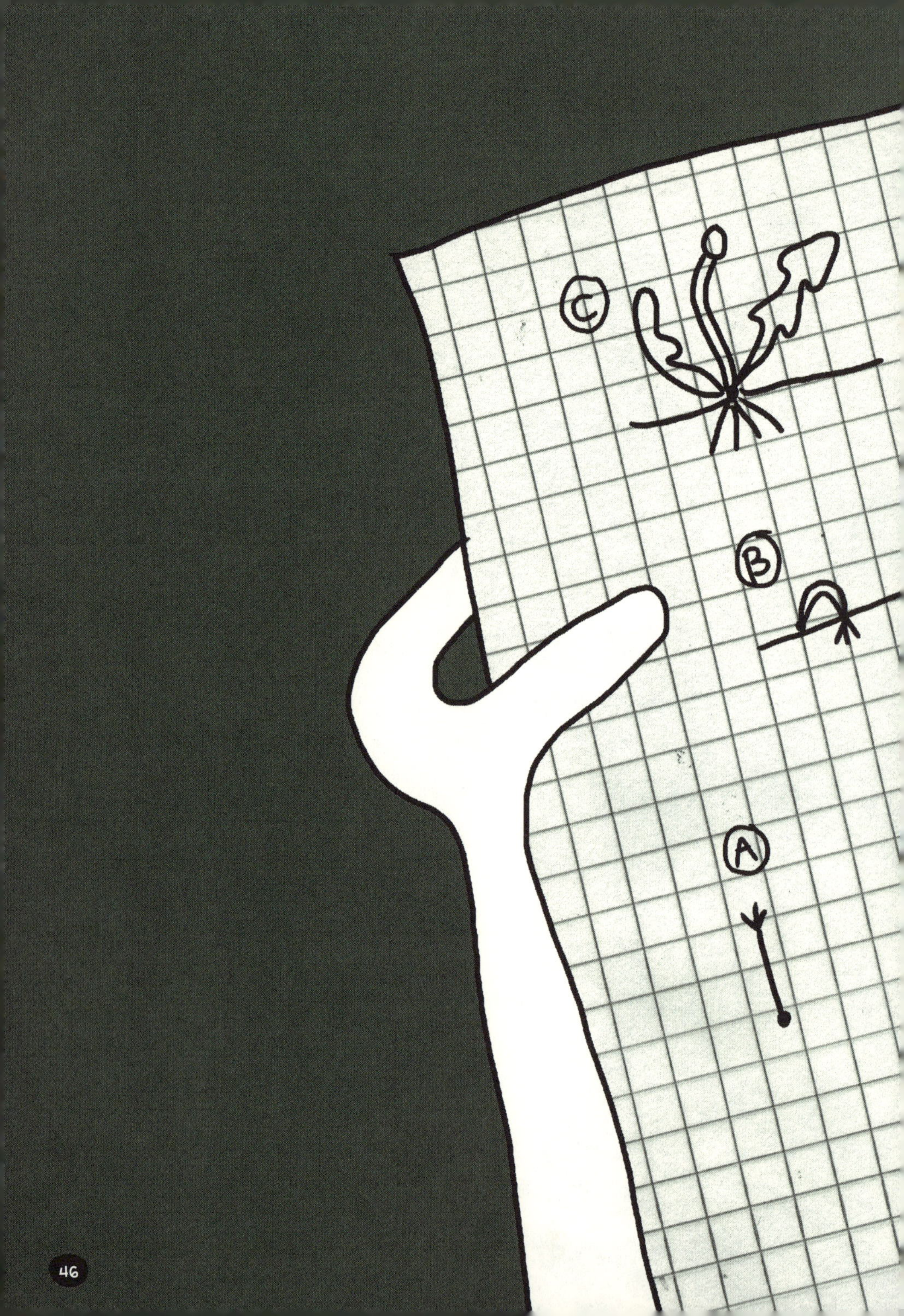
C
B
A

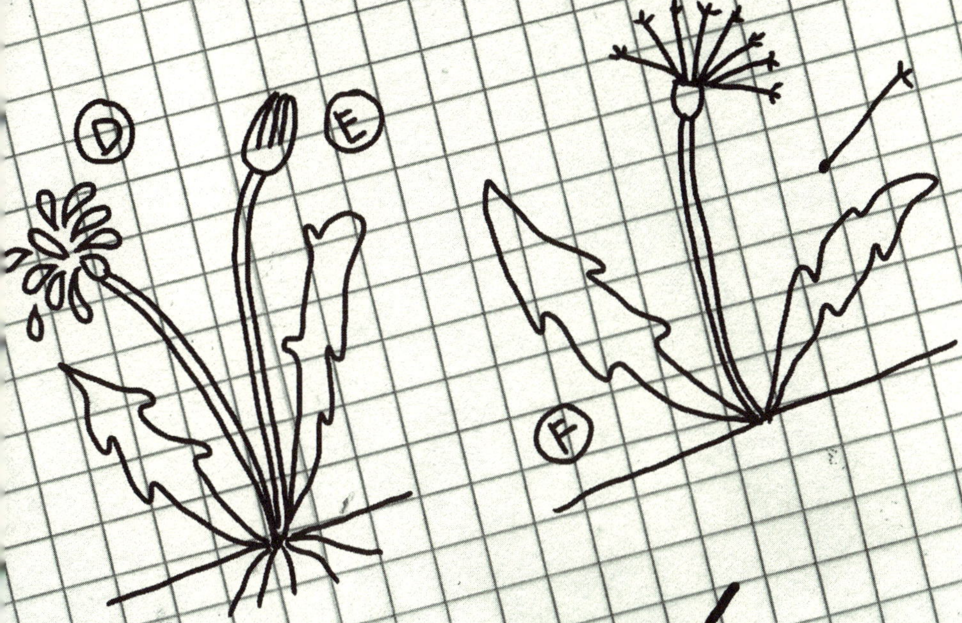
D
E
F

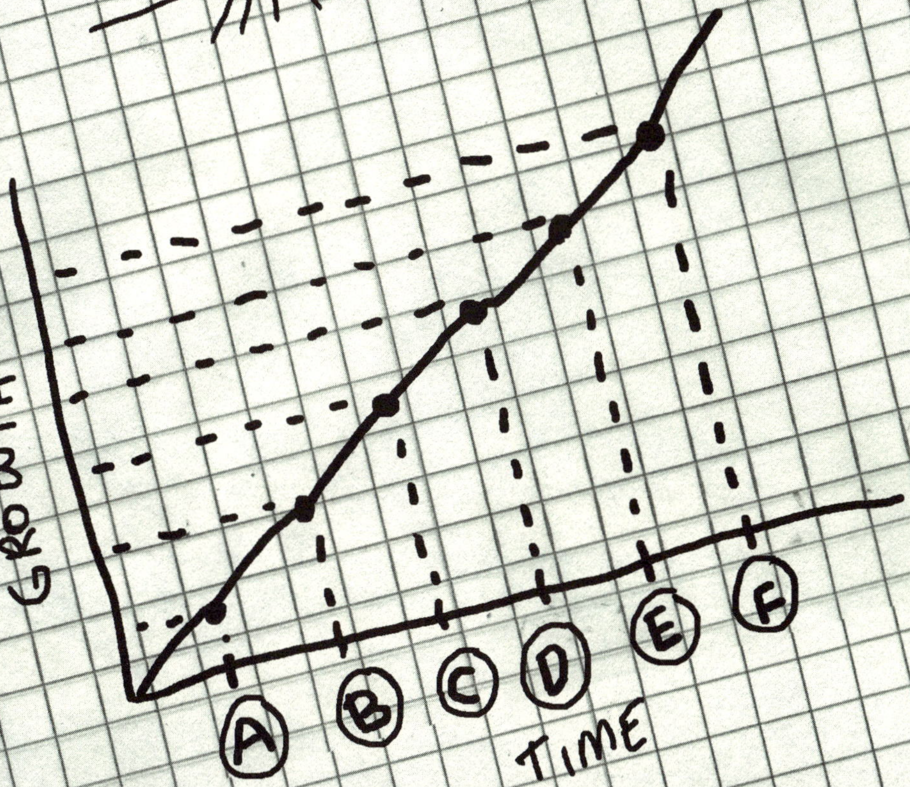
GROWTH
TIME
A
B
C
D
E
F

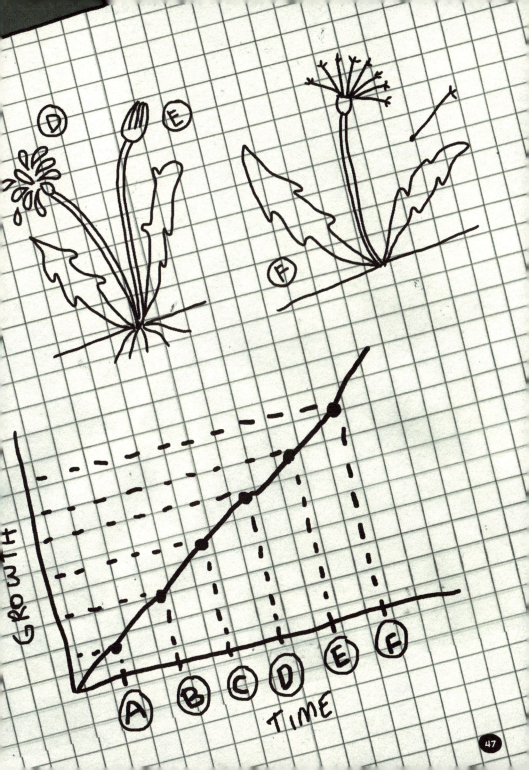

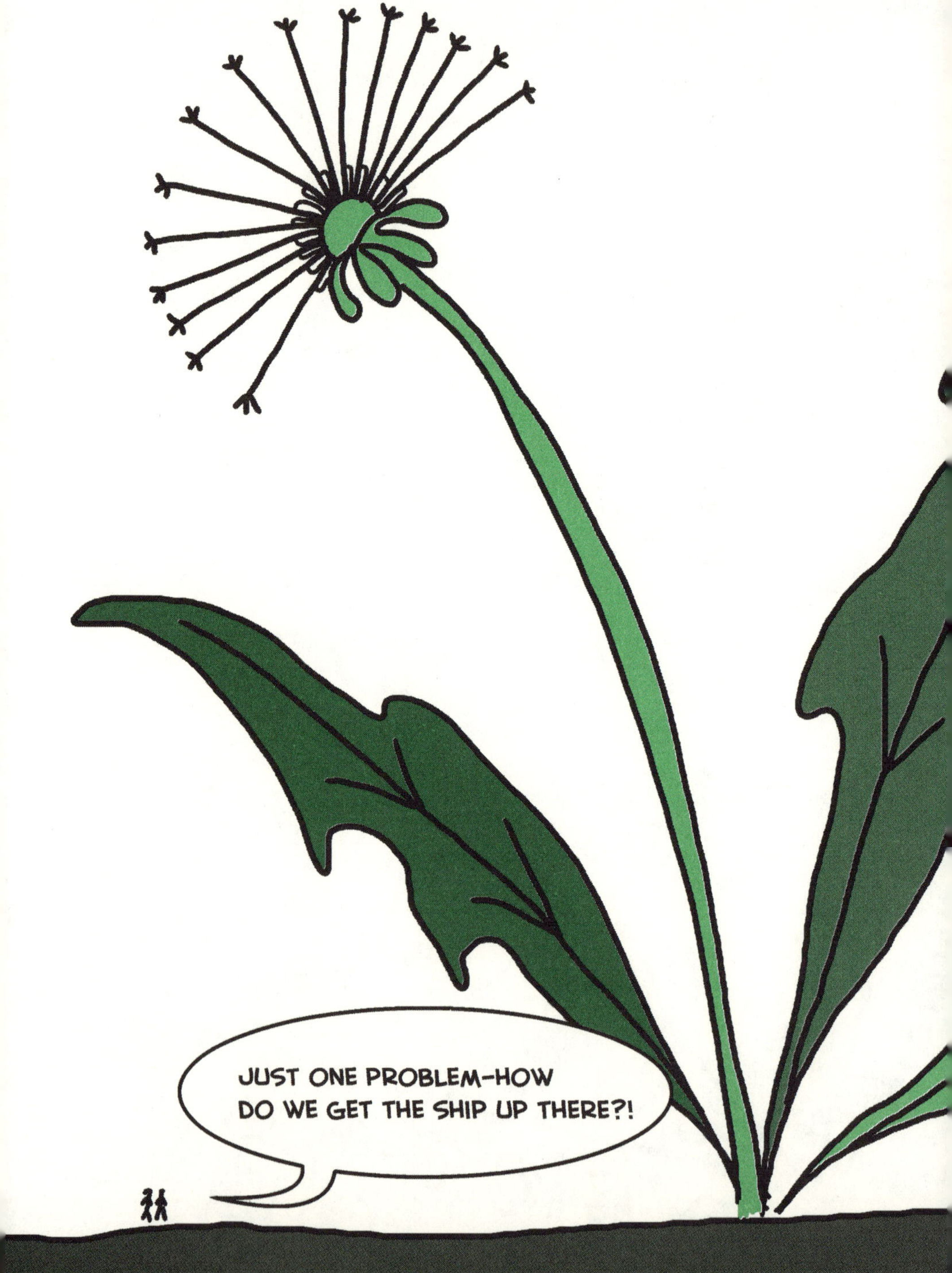
JUST ONE PROBLEM–HOW DO WE GET THE SHIP UP THERE?!

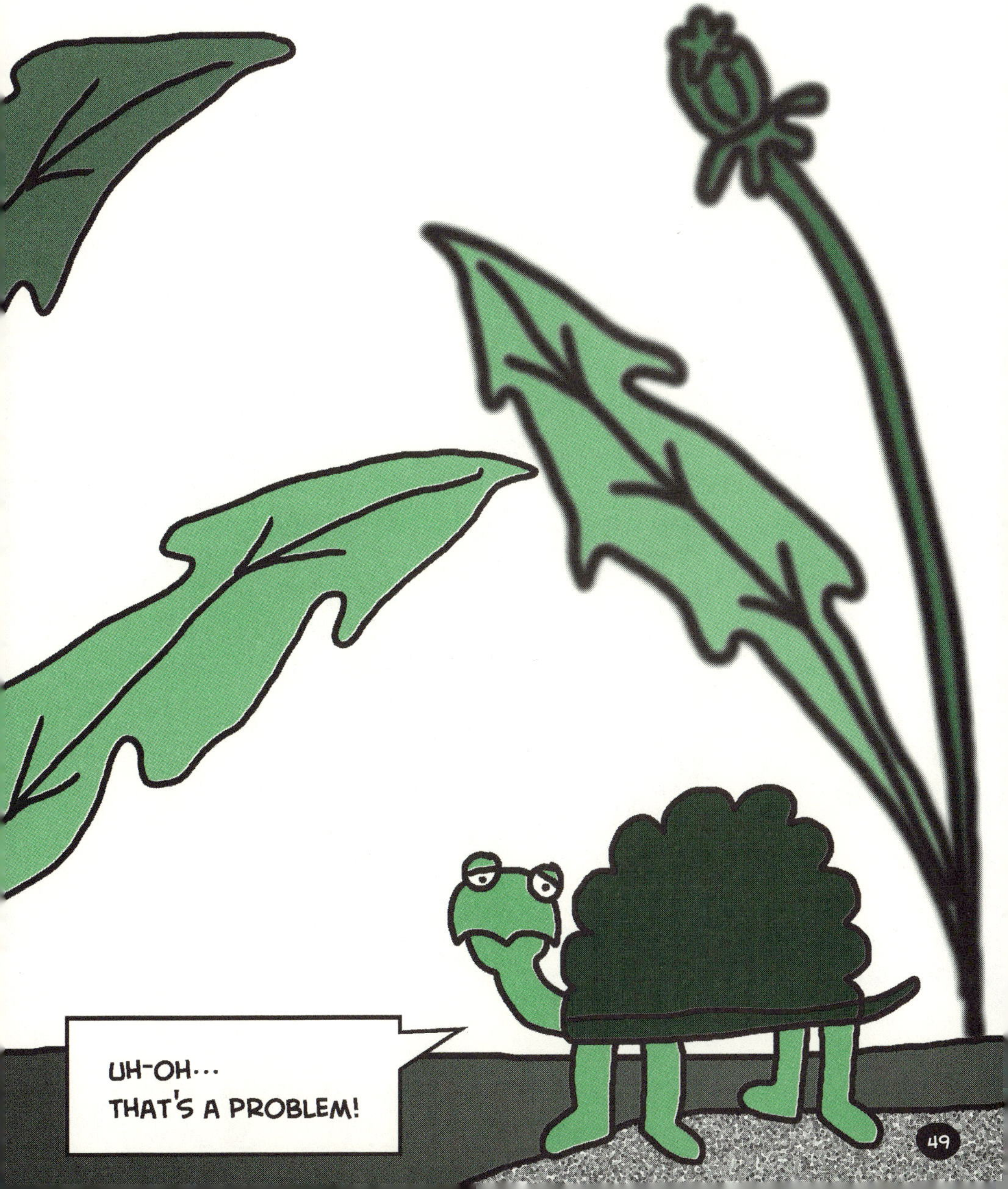
UH-OH...
THAT'S A PROBLEM!

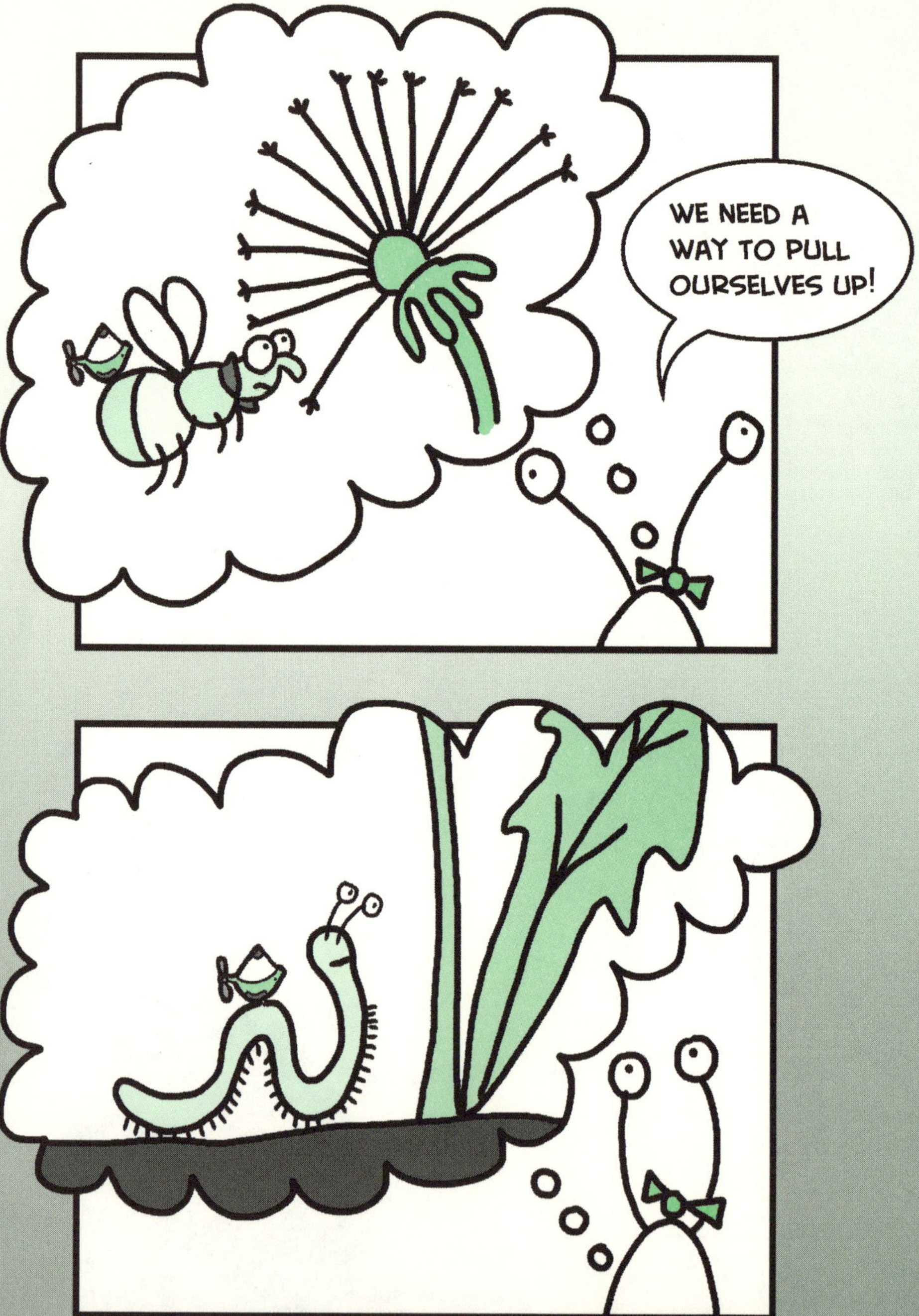
WE NEED A WAY TO PULL OURSELVES UP!

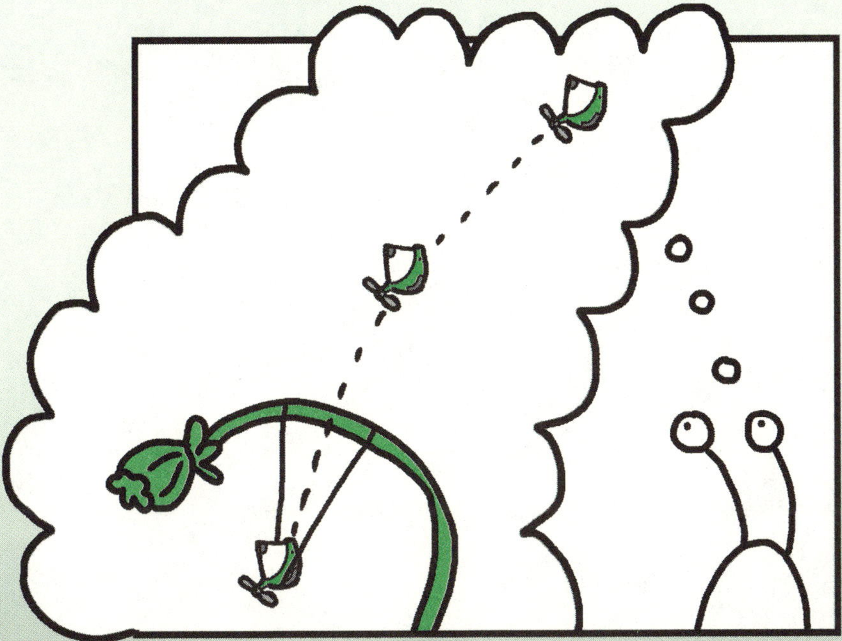

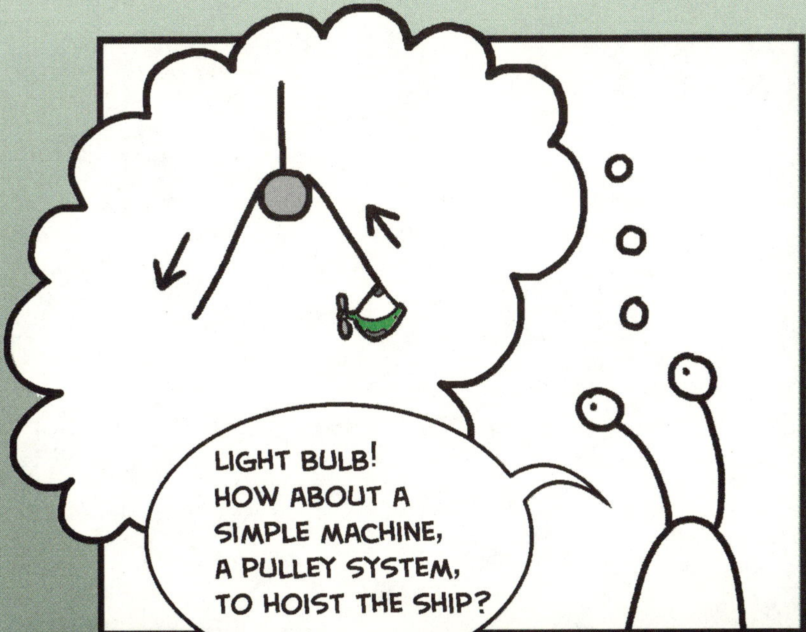
LIGHT BULB!
HOW ABOUT A
SIMPLE MACHINE,
A PULLEY SYSTEM,
TO HOIST THE SHIP?

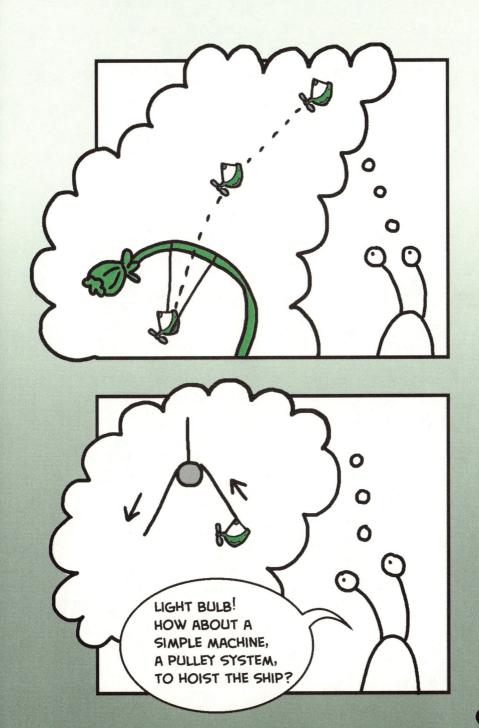

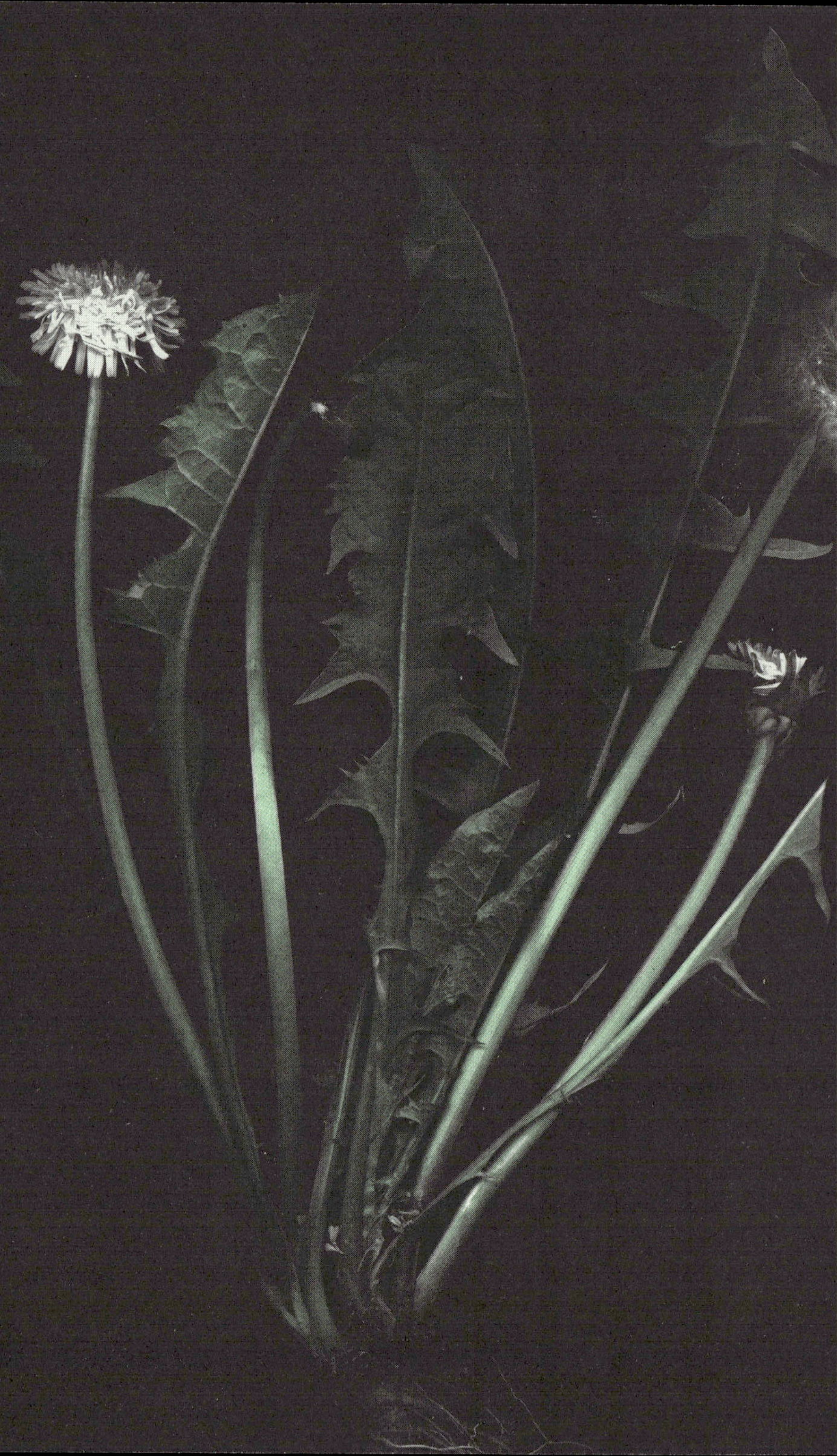

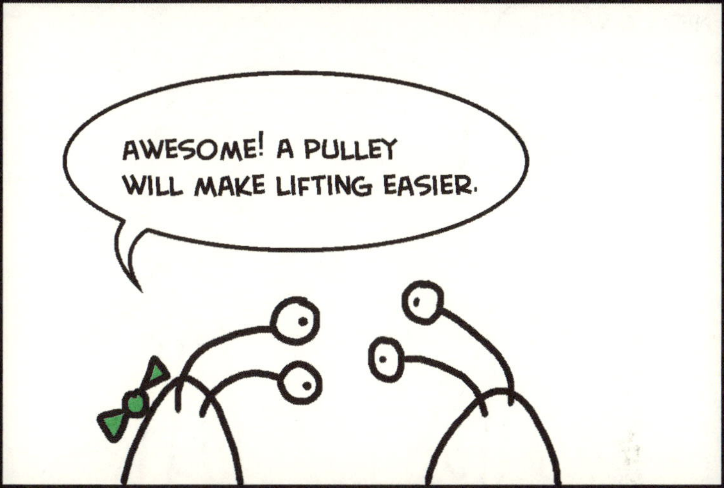
AWESOME! A PULLEY WILL MAKE LIFTING EASIER.

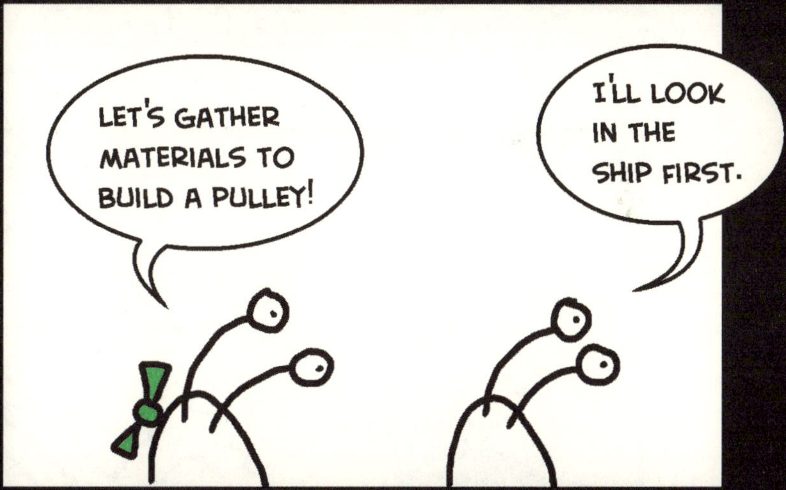
LET'S GATHER MATERIALS TO BUILD A PULLEY!
I'LL LOOK IN THE SHIP FIRST.

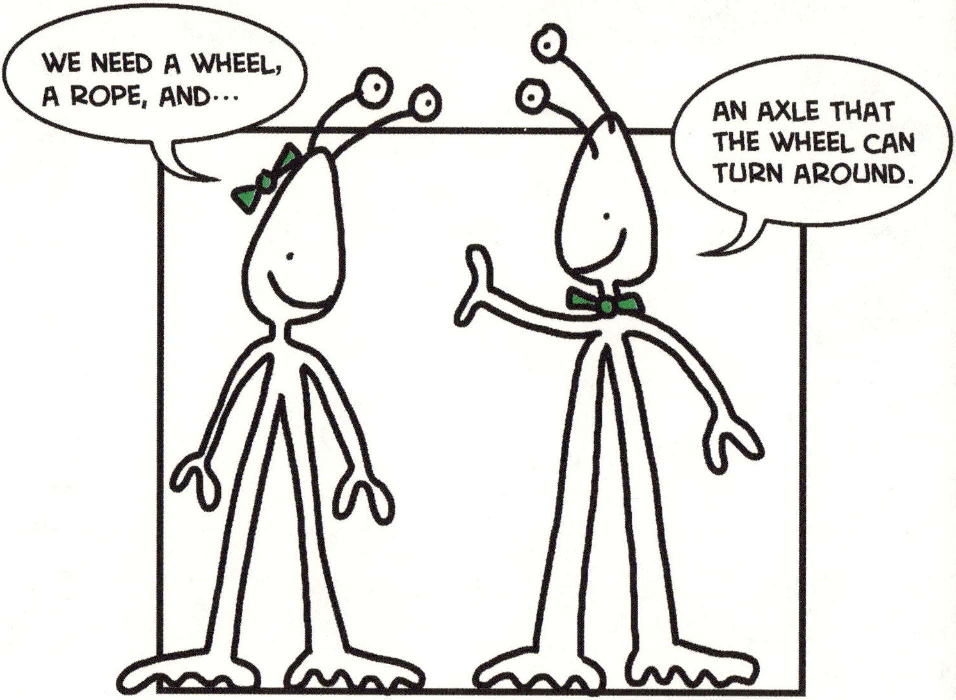
WE NEED A WHEEL, A ROPE, AND...
AN AXLE THAT THE WHEEL CAN TURN AROUND.

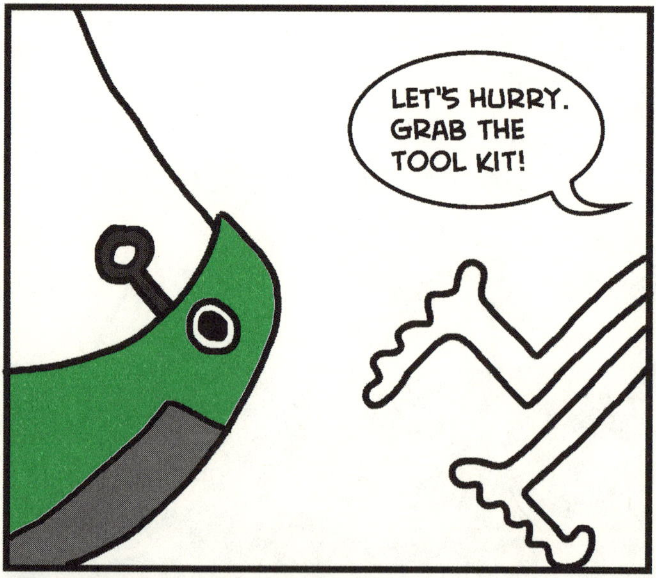
LET'S HURRY. GRAB THE TOOL KIT!

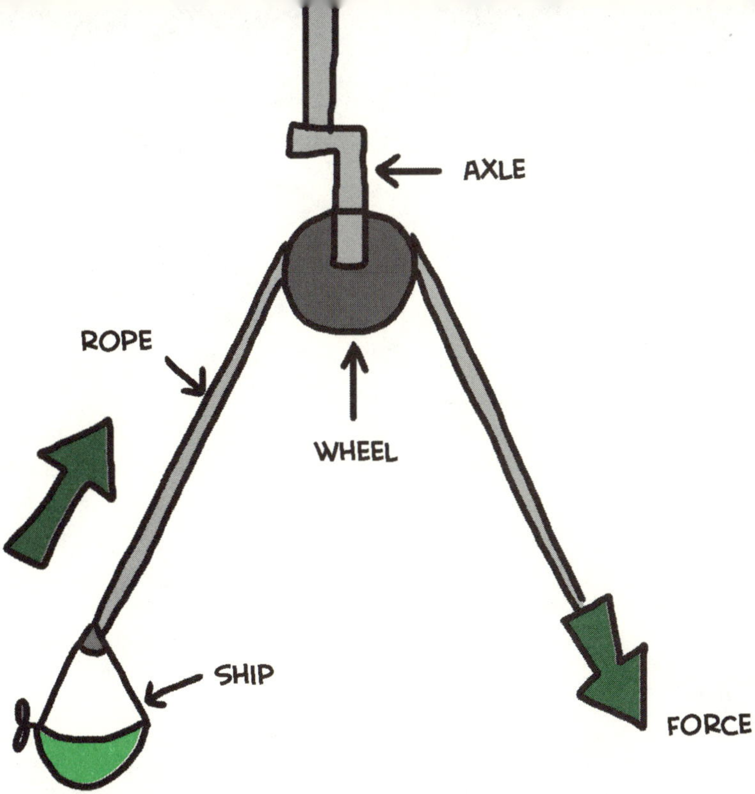
AXLE
ROPE
WHEEL
SHIP
FORCE

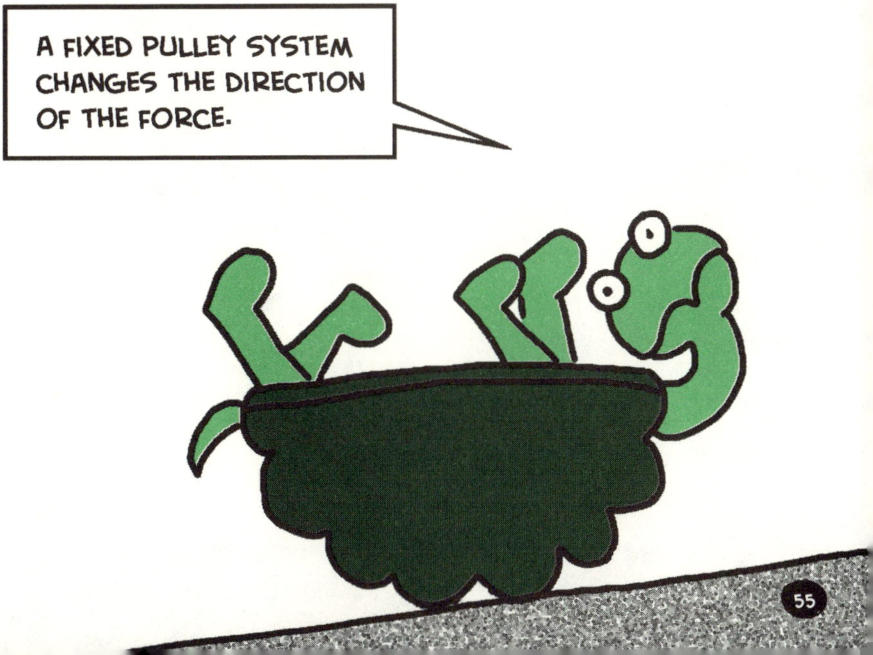
A FIXED PULLEY SYSTEM CHANGES THE DIRECTION OF THE FORCE.

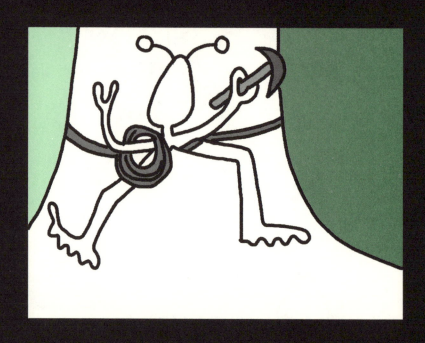

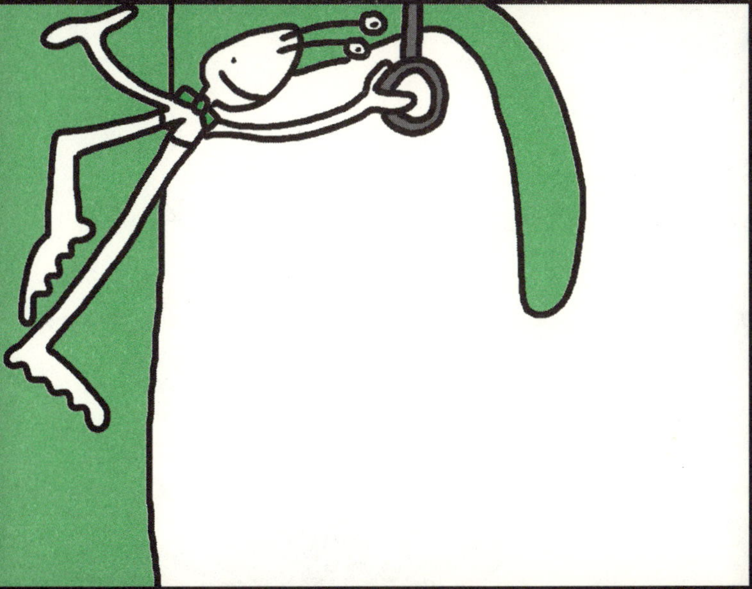

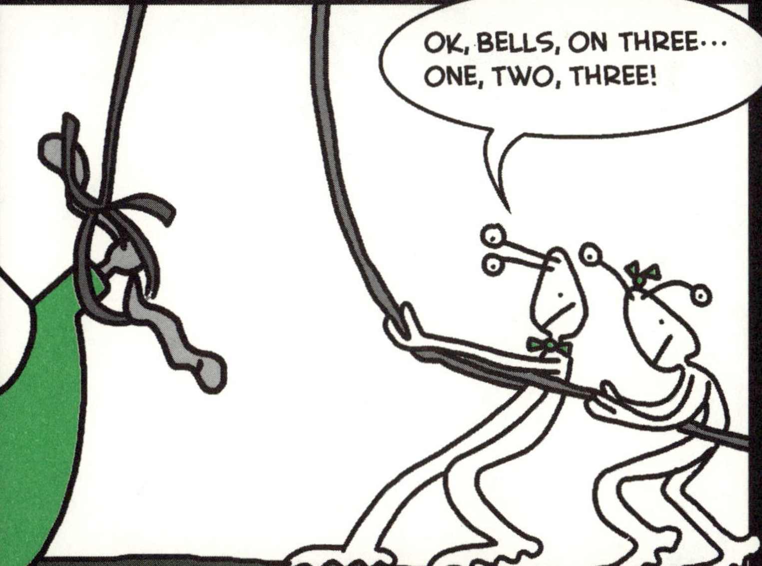
OK, BELLS, ON THREE... ONE, TWO, THREE!

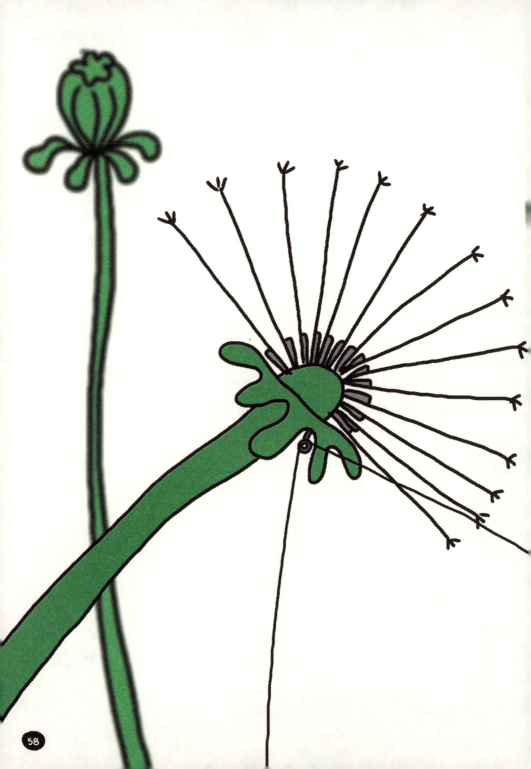

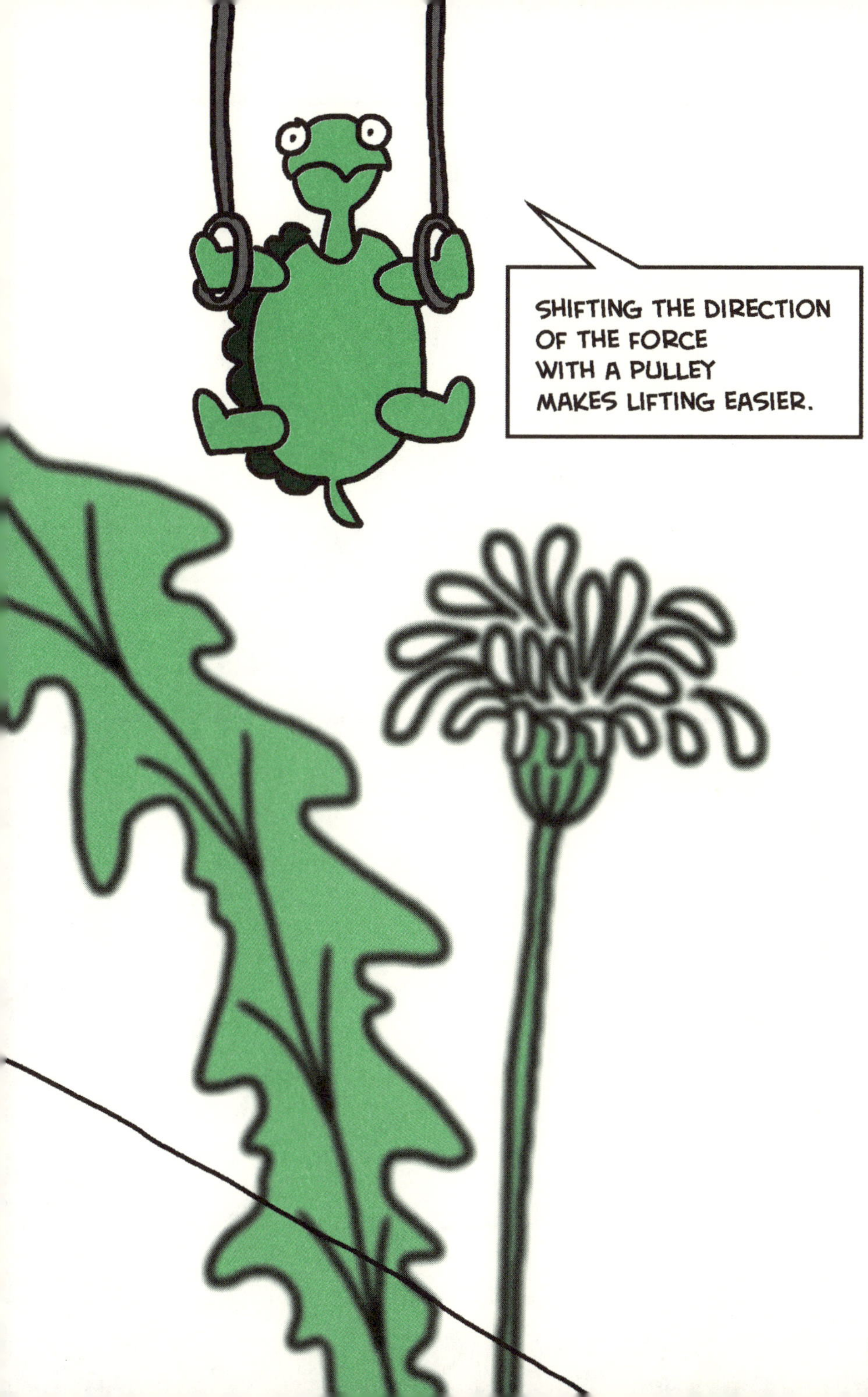
SHIFTING THE DIRECTION
OF THE FORCE
WITH A PULLEY
MAKES LIFTING EASIER.

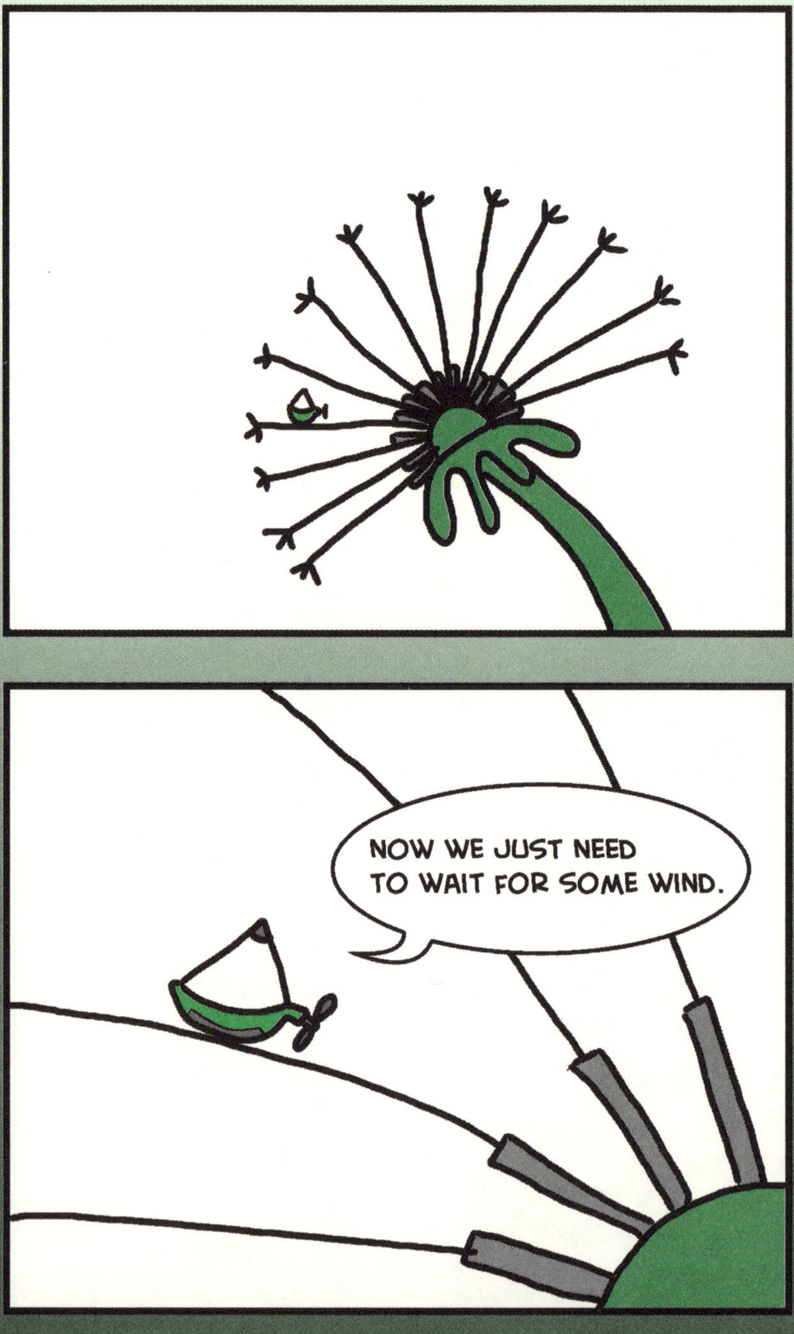
NOW WE JUST NEED TO WAIT FOR SOME WIND.

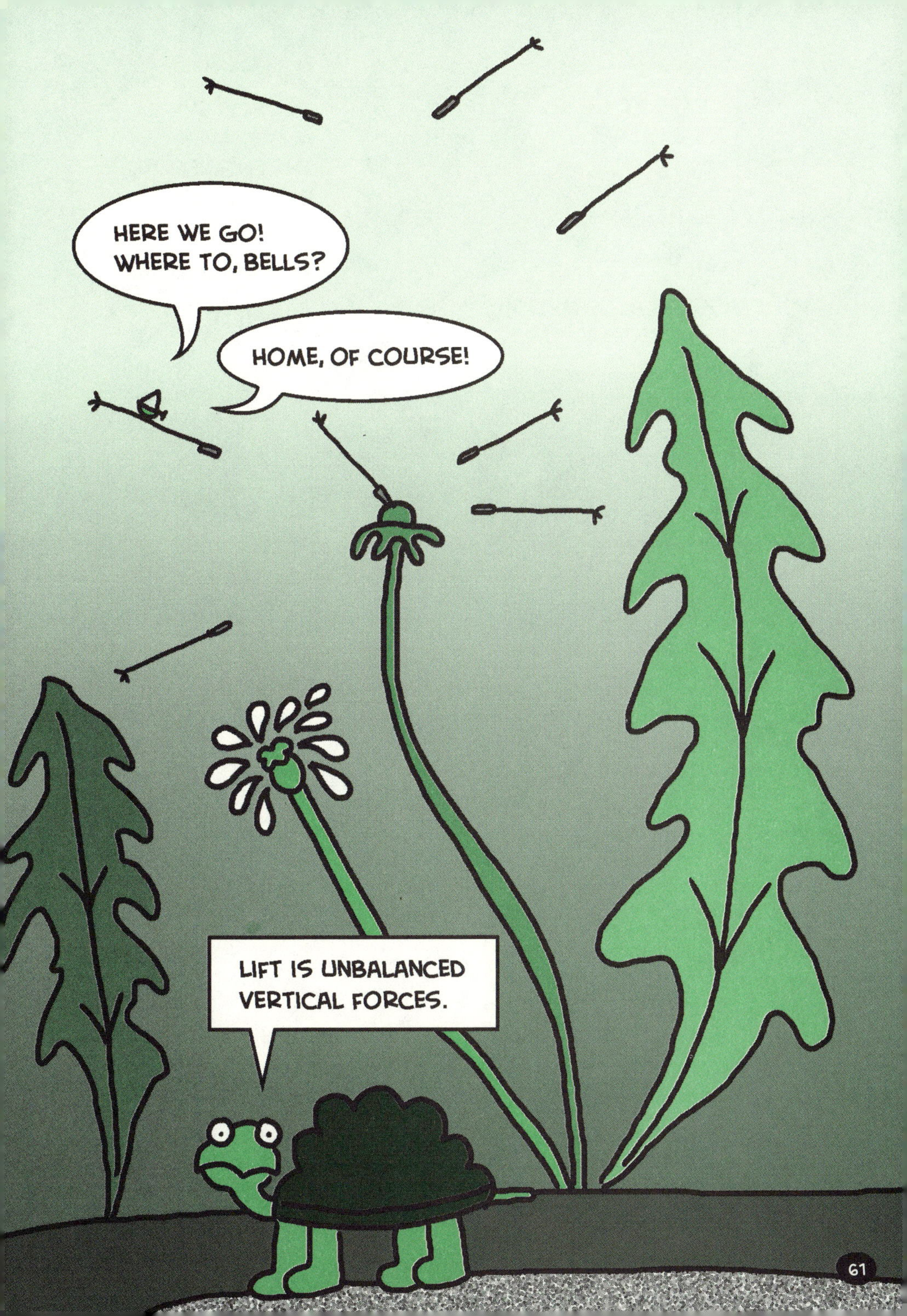
HERE WE GO!
WHERE TO, BELLS?
HOME, OF COURSE!
LIFT IS UNBALANCED
VERTICAL FORCES.

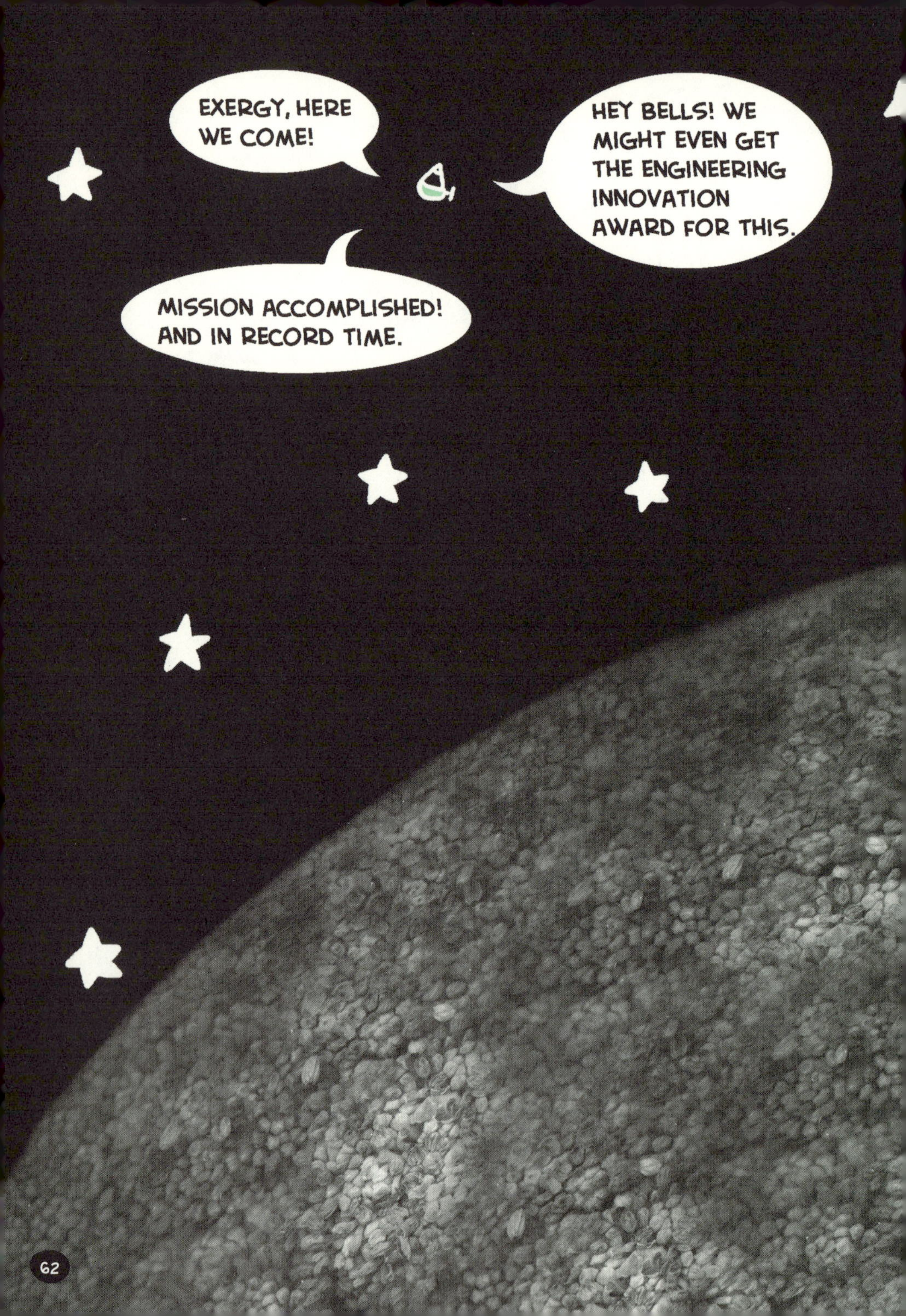
EXERGY, HERE WE COME!
HEY BELLS! WE MIGHT EVEN GET THE ENGINEERING INNOVATION AWARD FOR THIS.
MISSION ACCOMPLISHED! AND IN RECORD TIME.

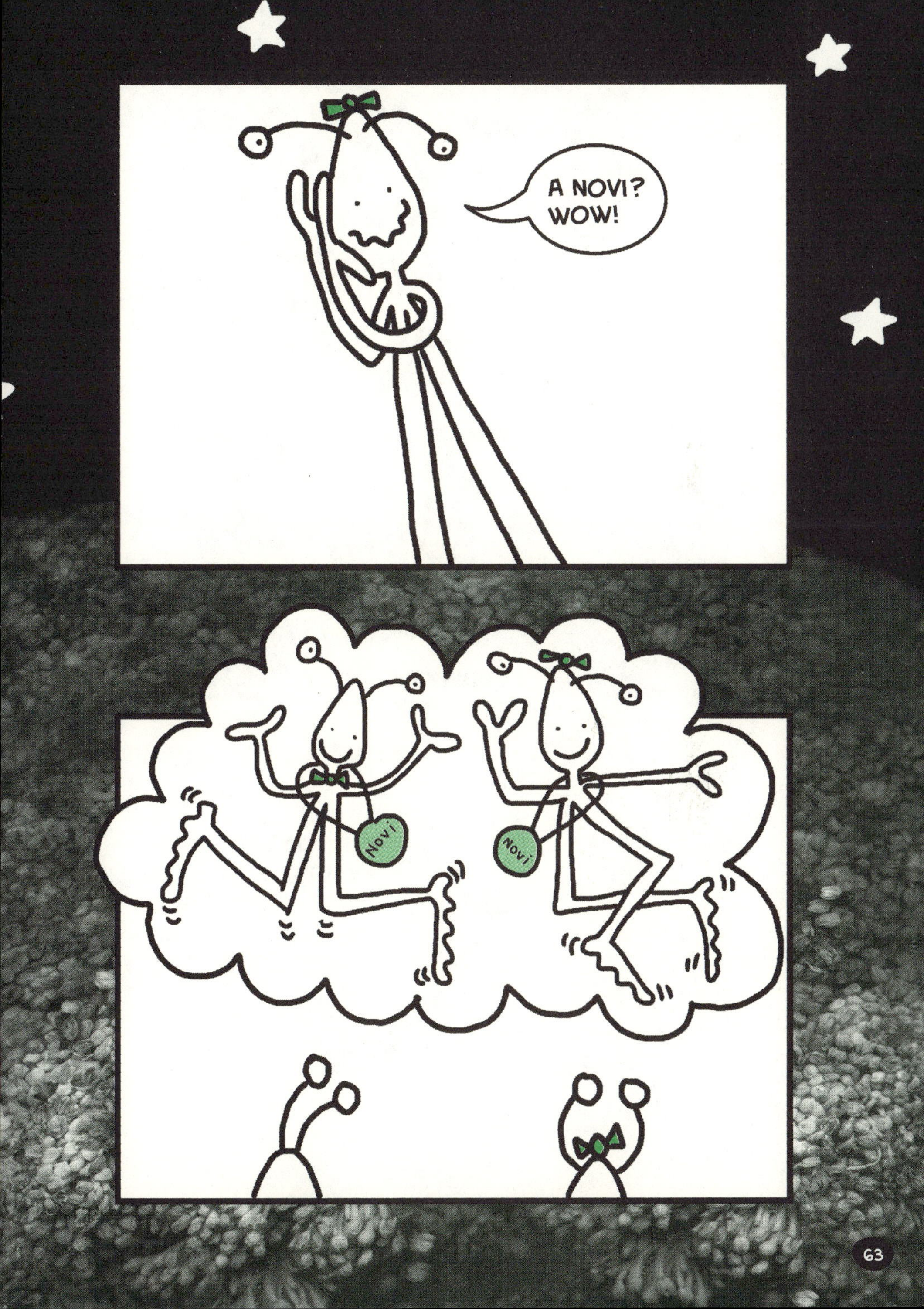
A NOVI?
WOW!
Novi
Novi

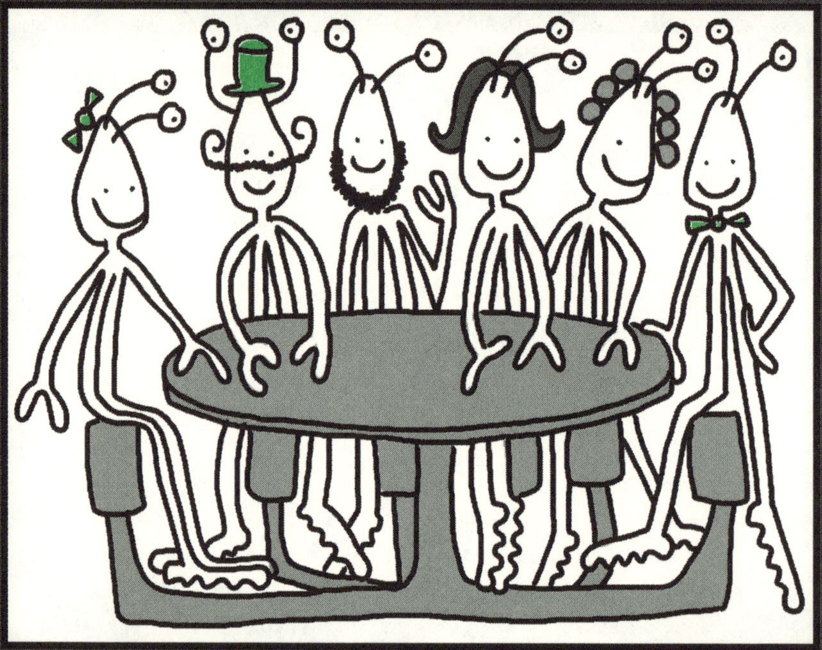

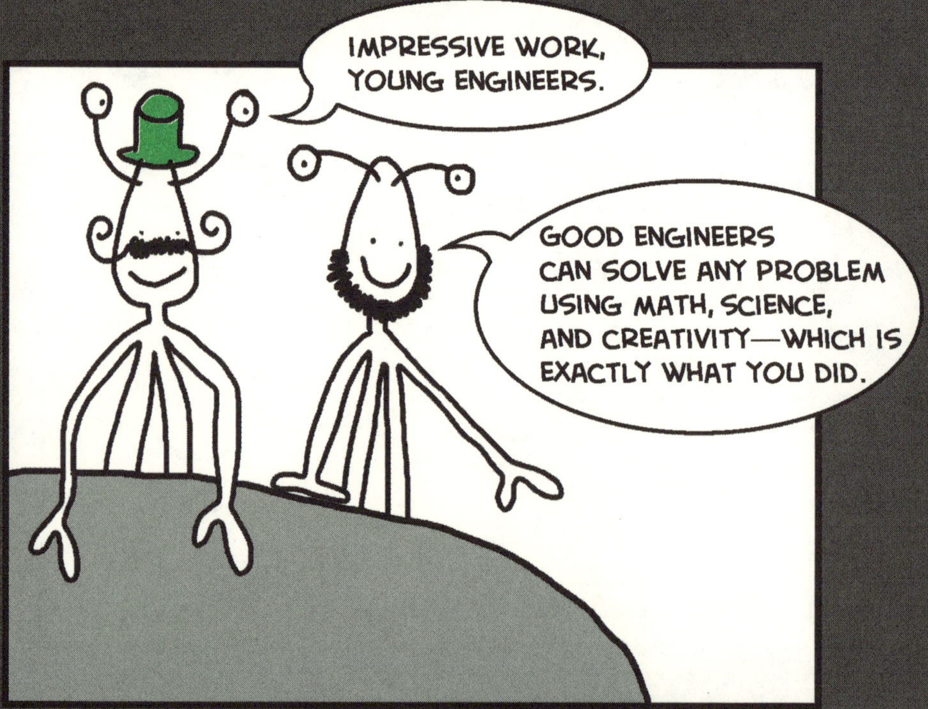
IMPRESSIVE WORK, YOUNG ENGINEERS.
GOOD ENGINEERS CAN SOLVE ANY PROBLEM USING MATH, SCIENCE, AND CREATIVITY—WHICH IS EXACTLY WHAT YOU DID.

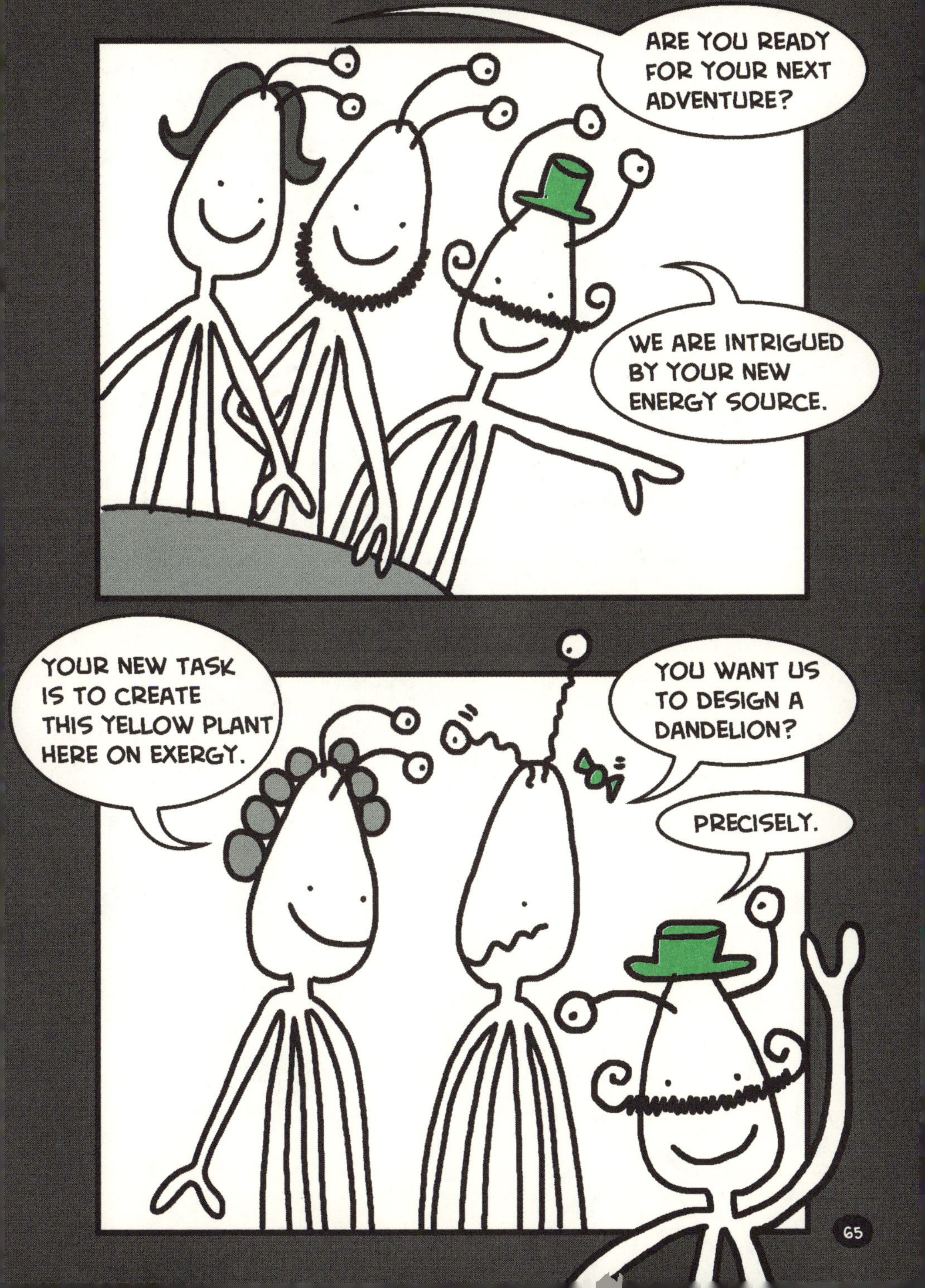
ARE YOU READY FOR YOUR NEXT ADVENTURE?
WE ARE INTRIGUED BY YOUR NEW ENERGY SOURCE.
YOUR NEW TASK IS TO CREATE THIS YELLOW PLANT HERE ON EXERGY.
YOU WANT US TO DESIGN A DANDELION?
PRECISELY.

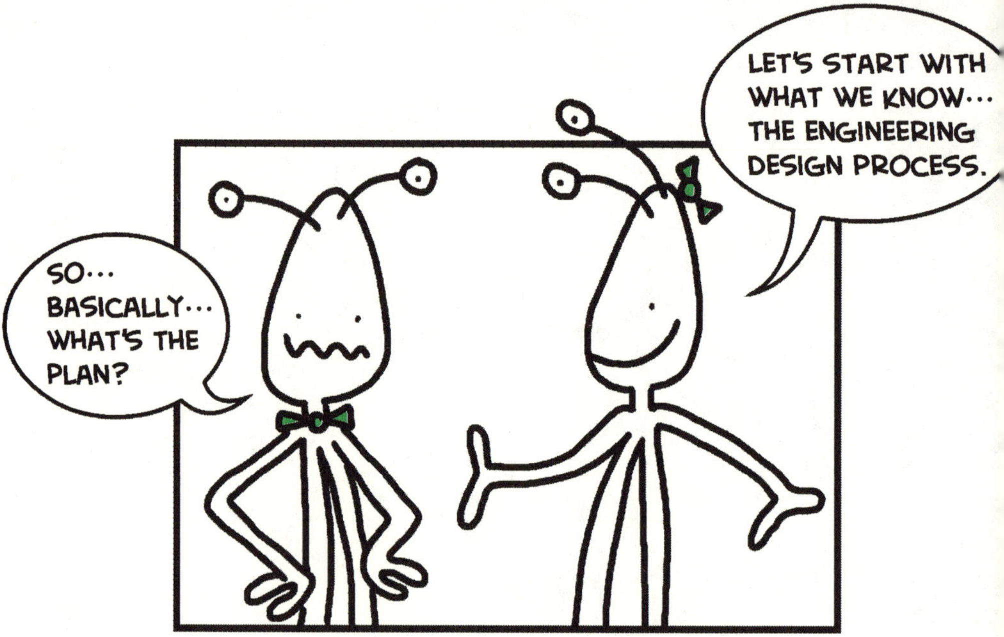
SO... BASICALLY... WHAT'S THE PLAN?
LET'S START WITH WHAT WE KNOW... THE ENGINEERING DESIGN PROCESS.

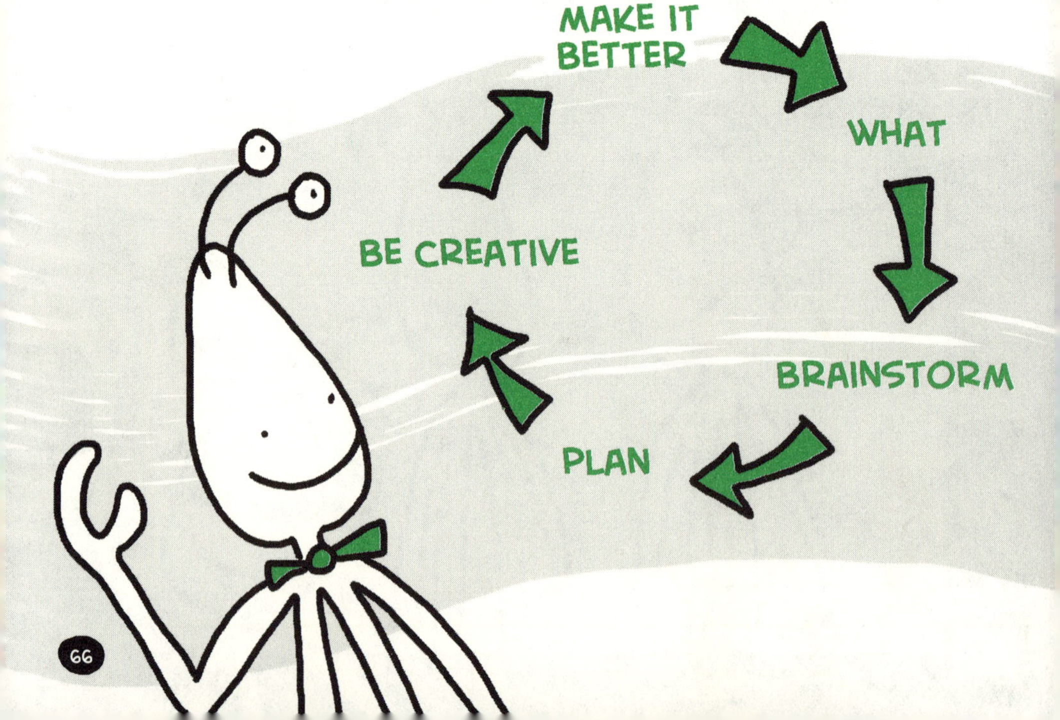
MAKE IT BETTER
WHAT
BRAINSTORM
PLAN
BE CREATIVE

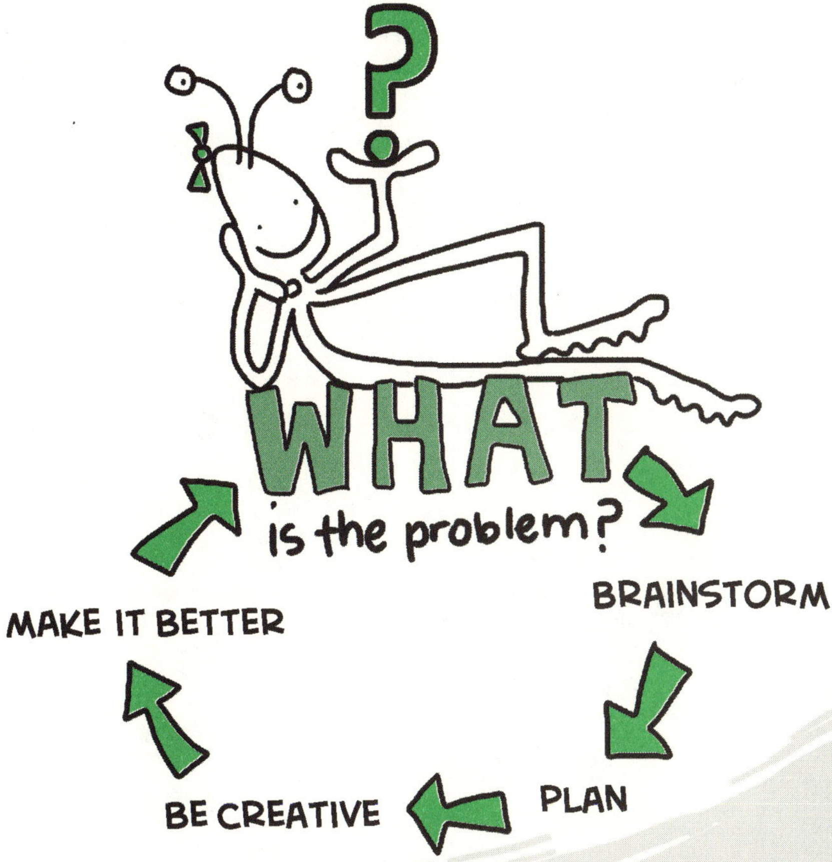
WHAT
is the problem?
BRAINSTORM
PLAN
BE CREATIVE
MAKE IT BETTER

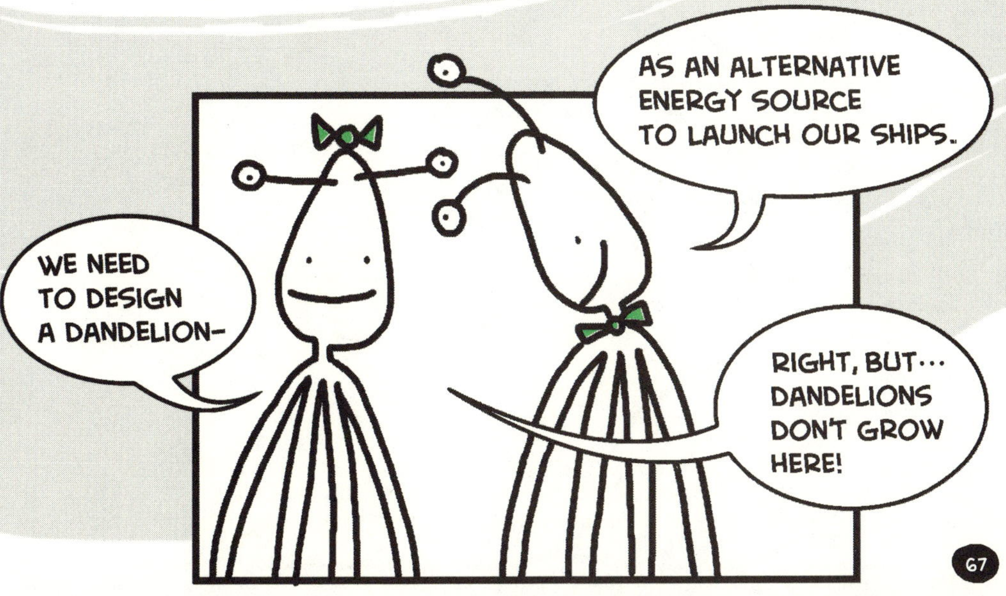
WE NEED TO DESIGN A DANDELION-
AS AN ALTERNATIVE ENERGY SOURCE TO LAUNCH OUR SHIPS..
RIGHT, BUT... DANDELIONS DON'T GROW HERE!

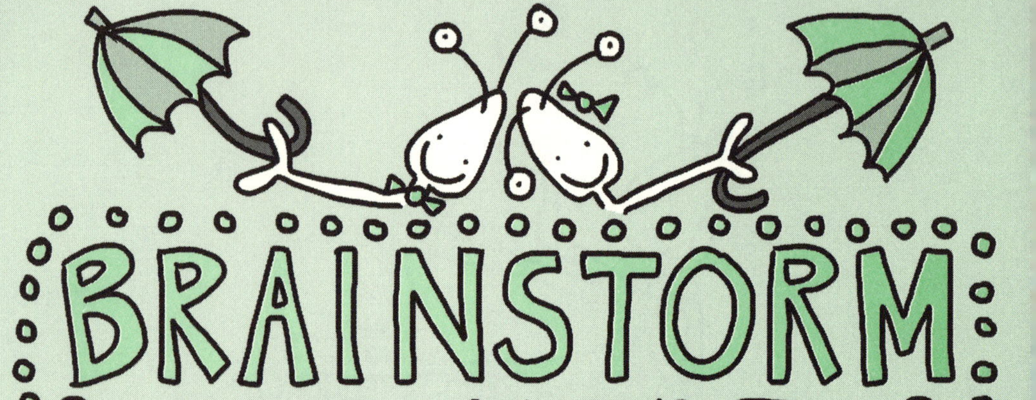

BRAINSTORM

POSSIBLE SOLUTIONS

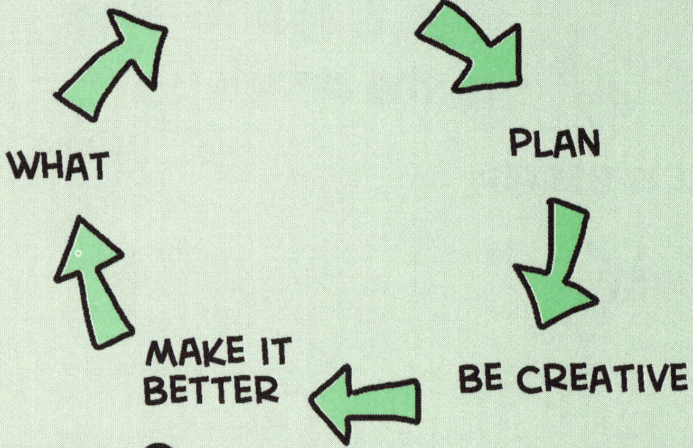

PLAN
BE CREATIVE
MAKE IT BETTER
WHAT

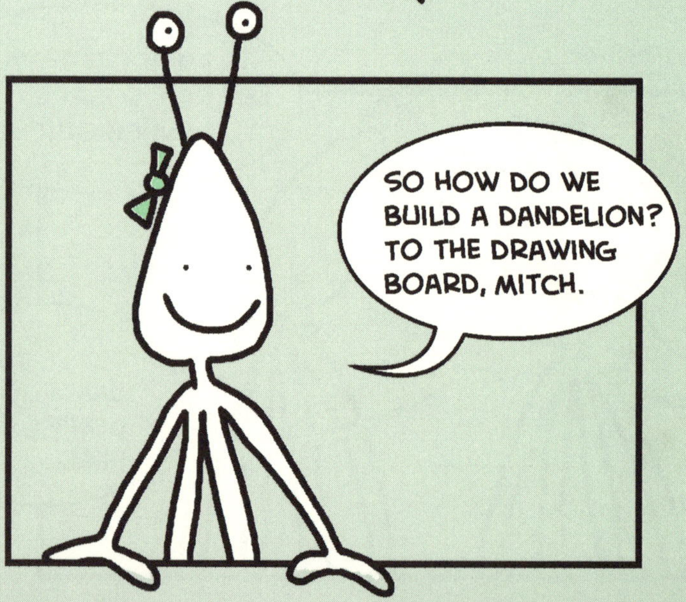

SO HOW DO WE BUILD A DANDELION? TO THE DRAWING BOARD, MITCH.

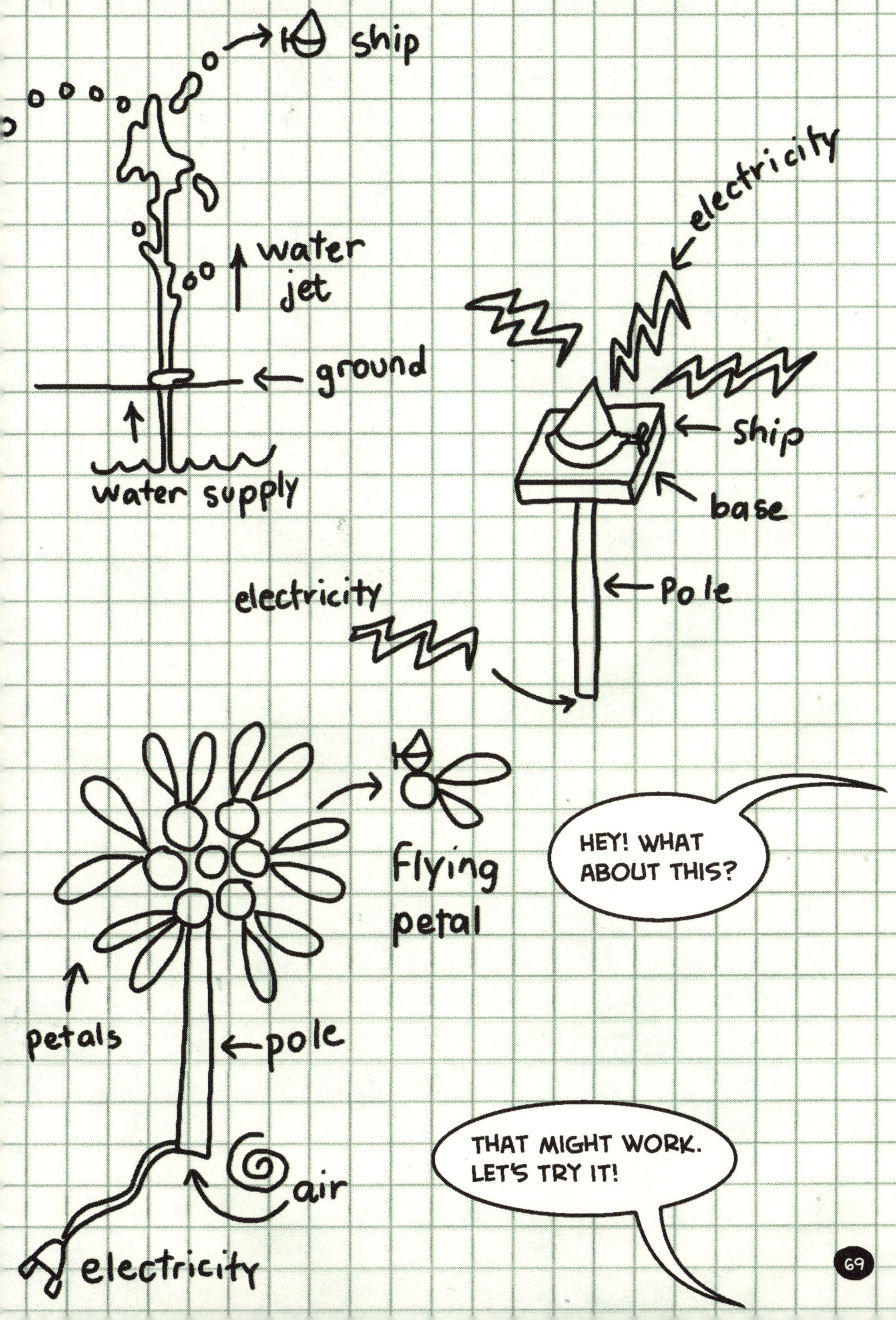
ship
water jet
ground
water supply
electricity
ship
base
Pole
electricity
Flying petal
petals
pole
air
electricity
HEY! WHAT ABOUT THIS?
THAT MIGHT WORK. LET'S TRY IT!

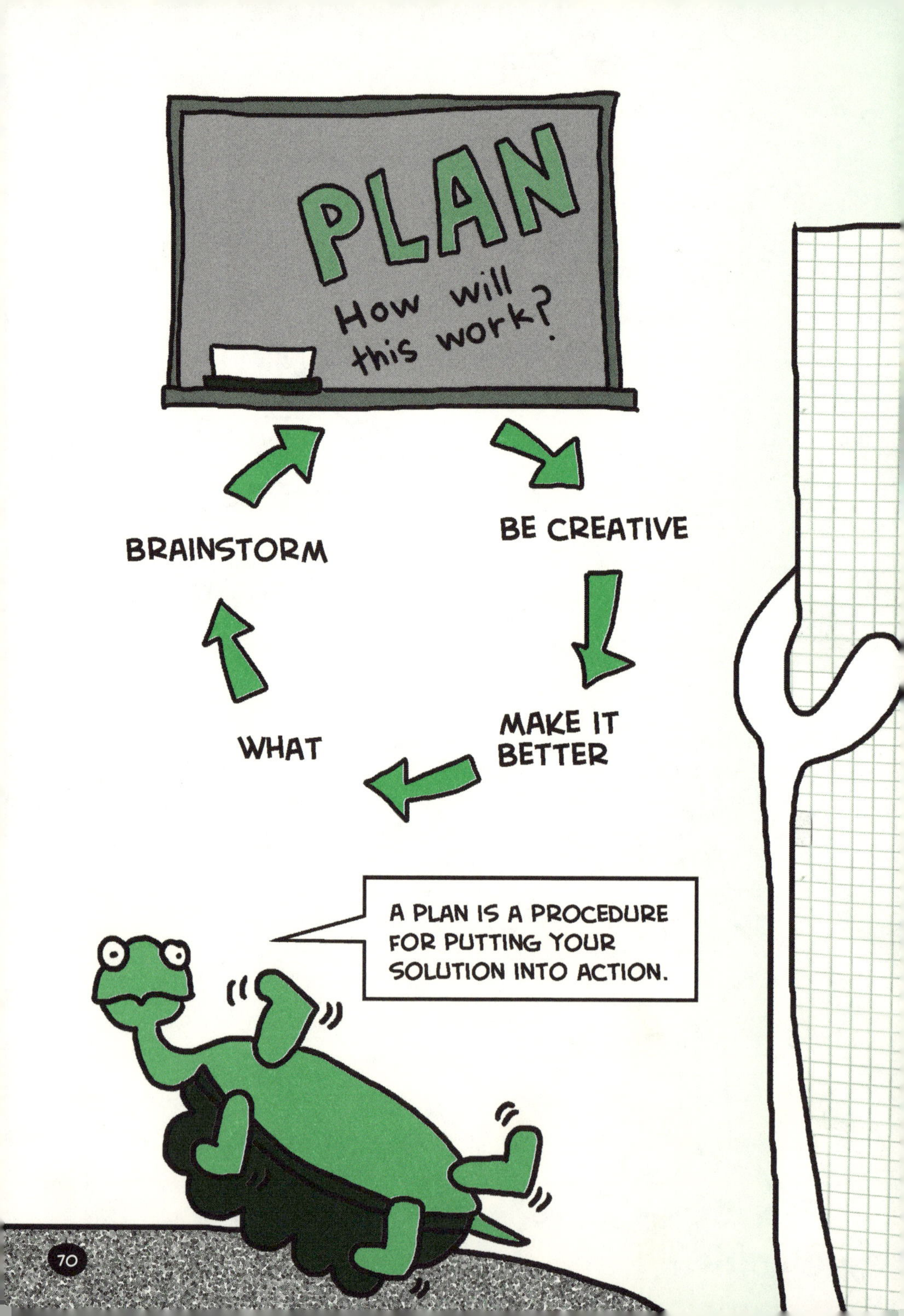
PLAN
How will this work?
BE CREATIVE
MAKE IT BETTER
WHAT
BRAINSTORM
A PLAN IS A PROCEDURE FOR PUTTING YOUR SOLUTION INTO ACTION.

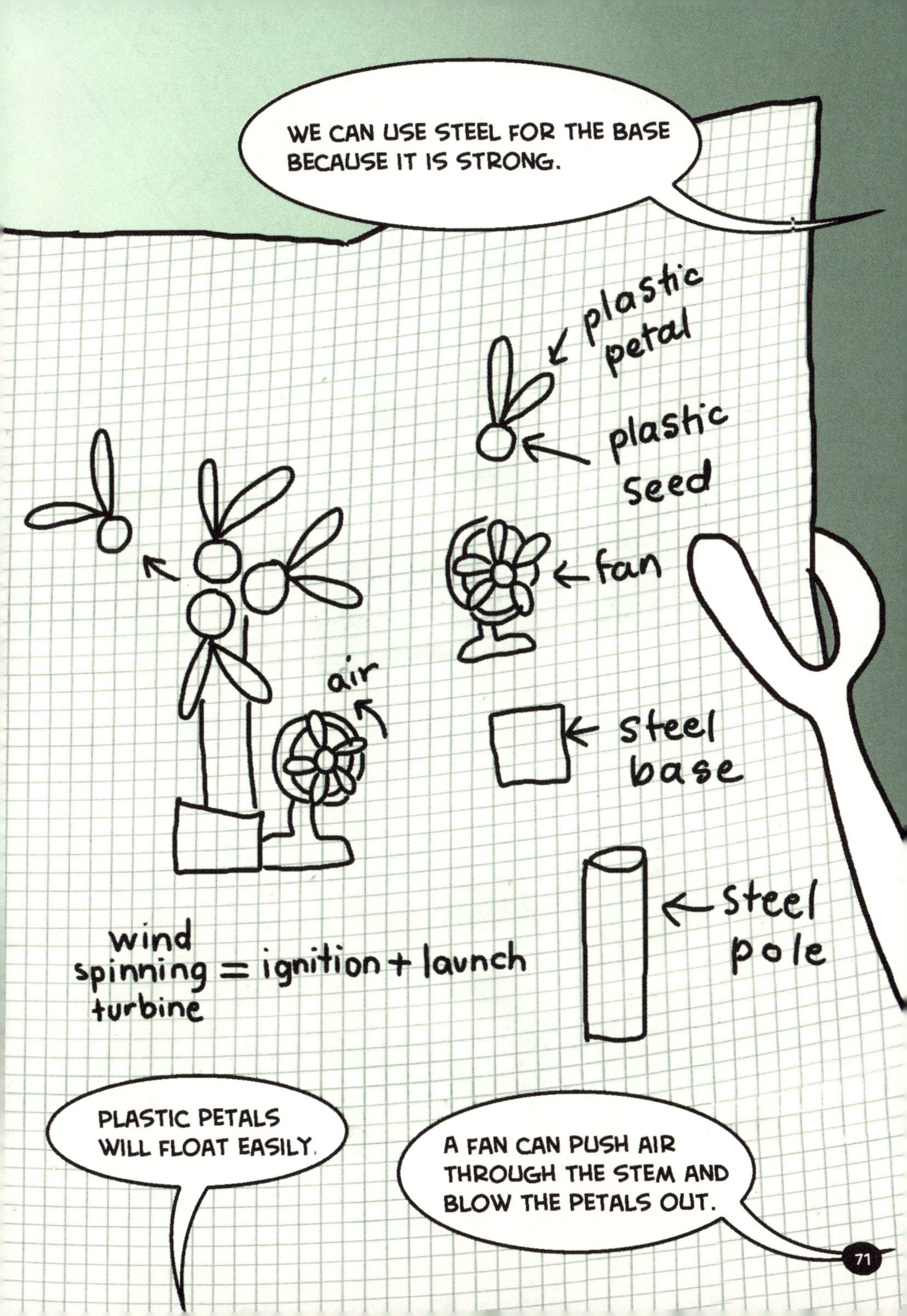

WE CAN USE STEEL FOR THE BASE BECAUSE IT IS STRONG.
plastic petal
plastic seed
fan
air
steel base
steel pole
wind spinning turbine = ignition + launch
PLASTIC PETALS WILL FLOAT EASILY.
A FAN CAN PUSH AIR THROUGH THE STEM AND BLOW THE PETALS OUT.

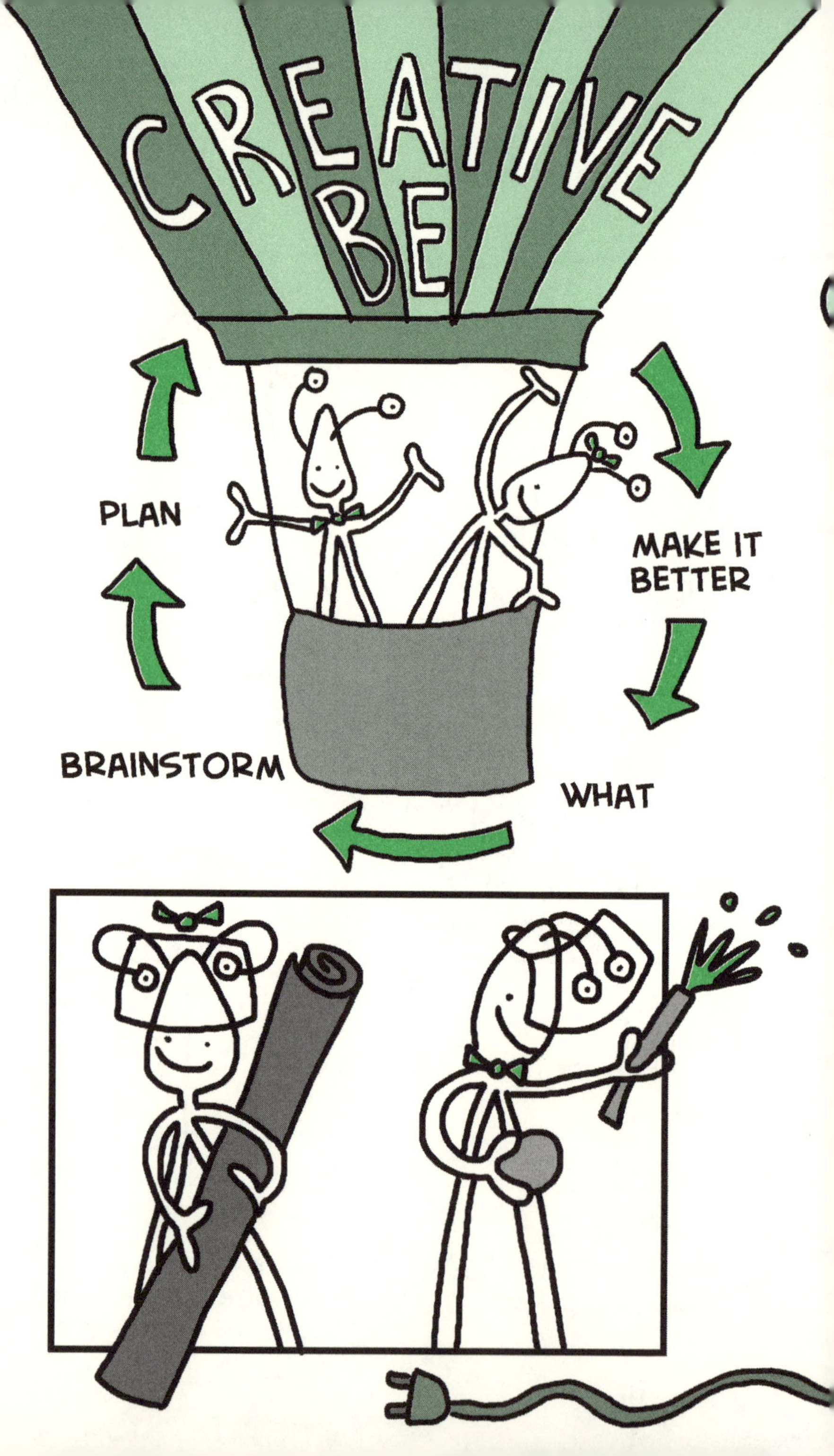
BE
CREATIVE
PLAN
MAKE IT BETTER
BRAINSTORM
WHAT

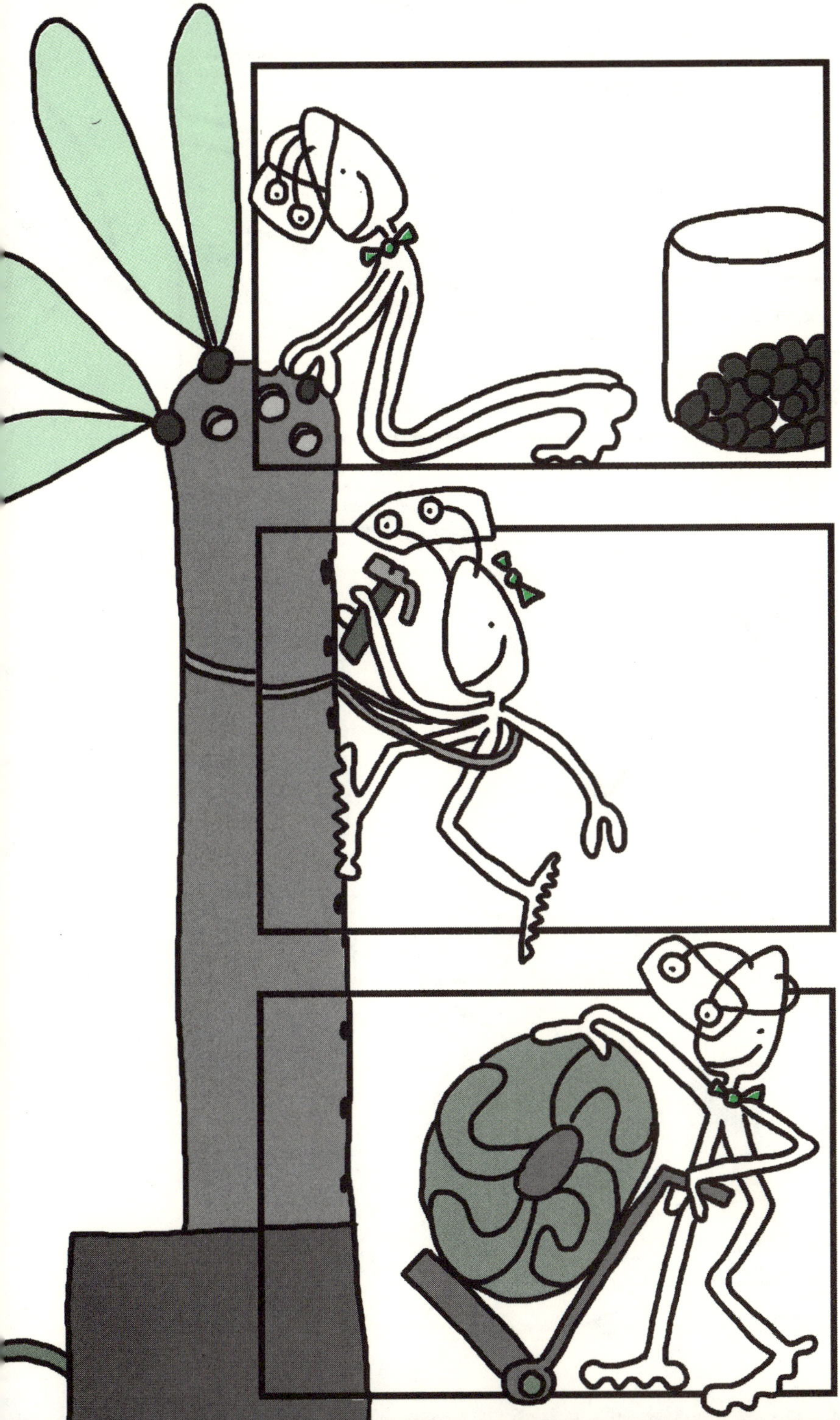

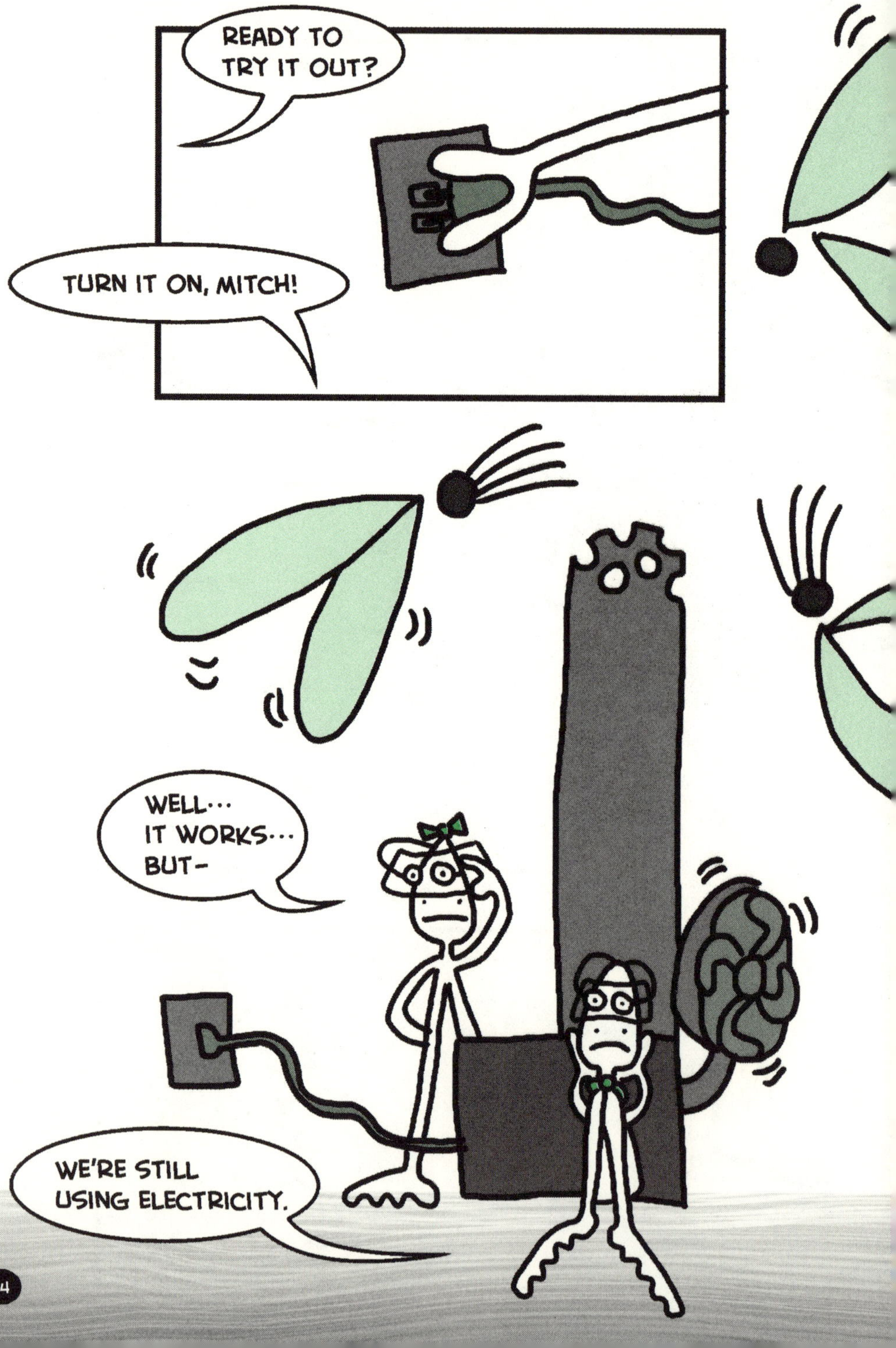
READY TO TRY IT OUT?
TURN IT ON, MITCH!
WELL... IT WORKS... BUT-
WE'RE STILL USING ELECTRICITY.

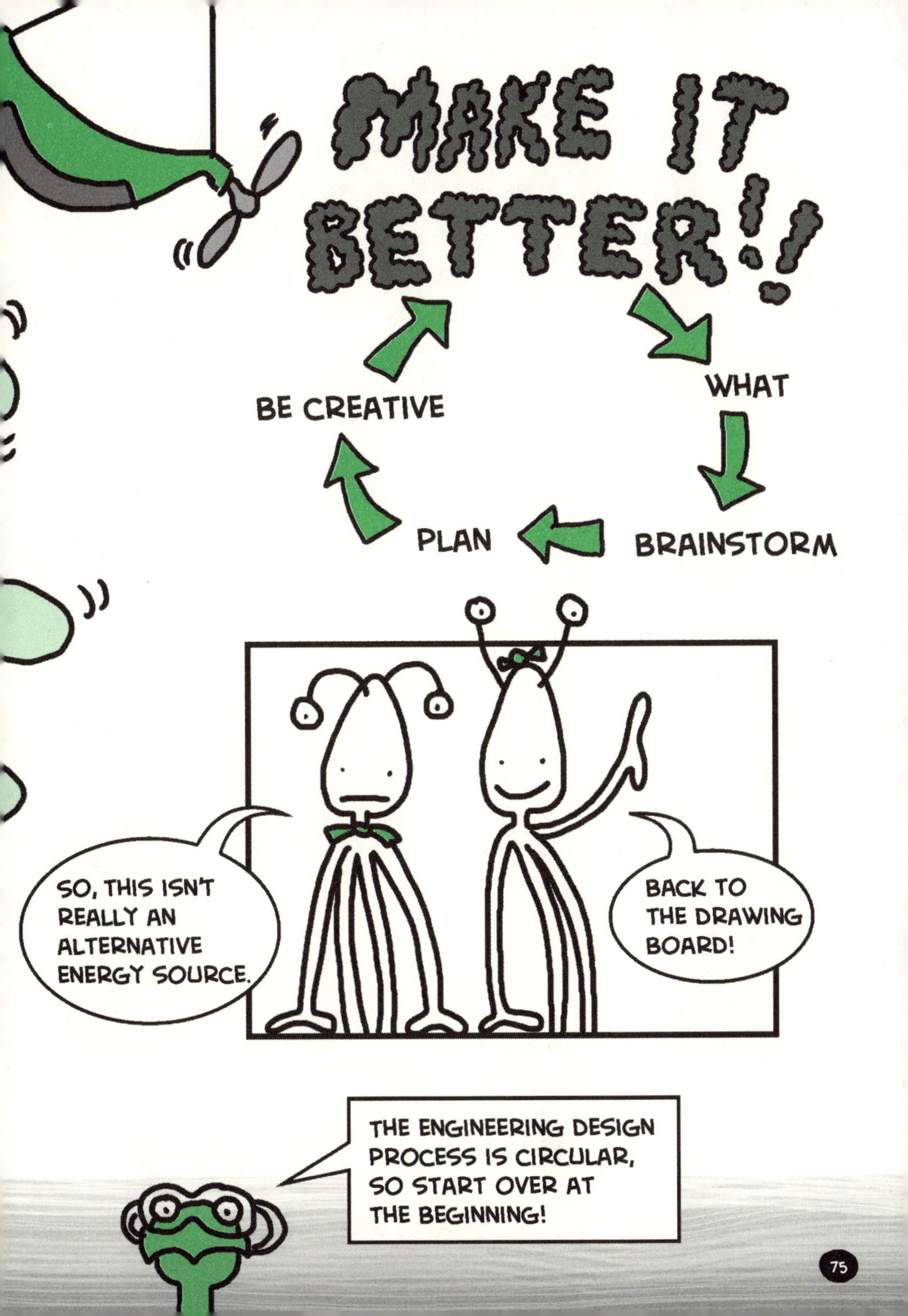
MAKE IT BETTER!!
WHAT
BRAINSTORM
PLAN
BE CREATIVE
SO, THIS ISN'T REALLY AN ALTERNATIVE ENERGY SOURCE.
BACK TO THE DRAWING BOARD!
THE ENGINEERING DESIGN PROCESS IS CIRCULAR, SO START OVER AT THE BEGINNING!

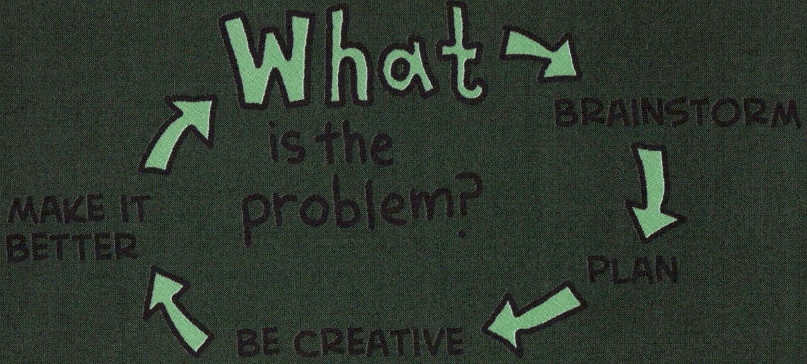
What is the problem?
BRAINSTORM
PLAN
BE CREATIVE
MAKE IT BETTER

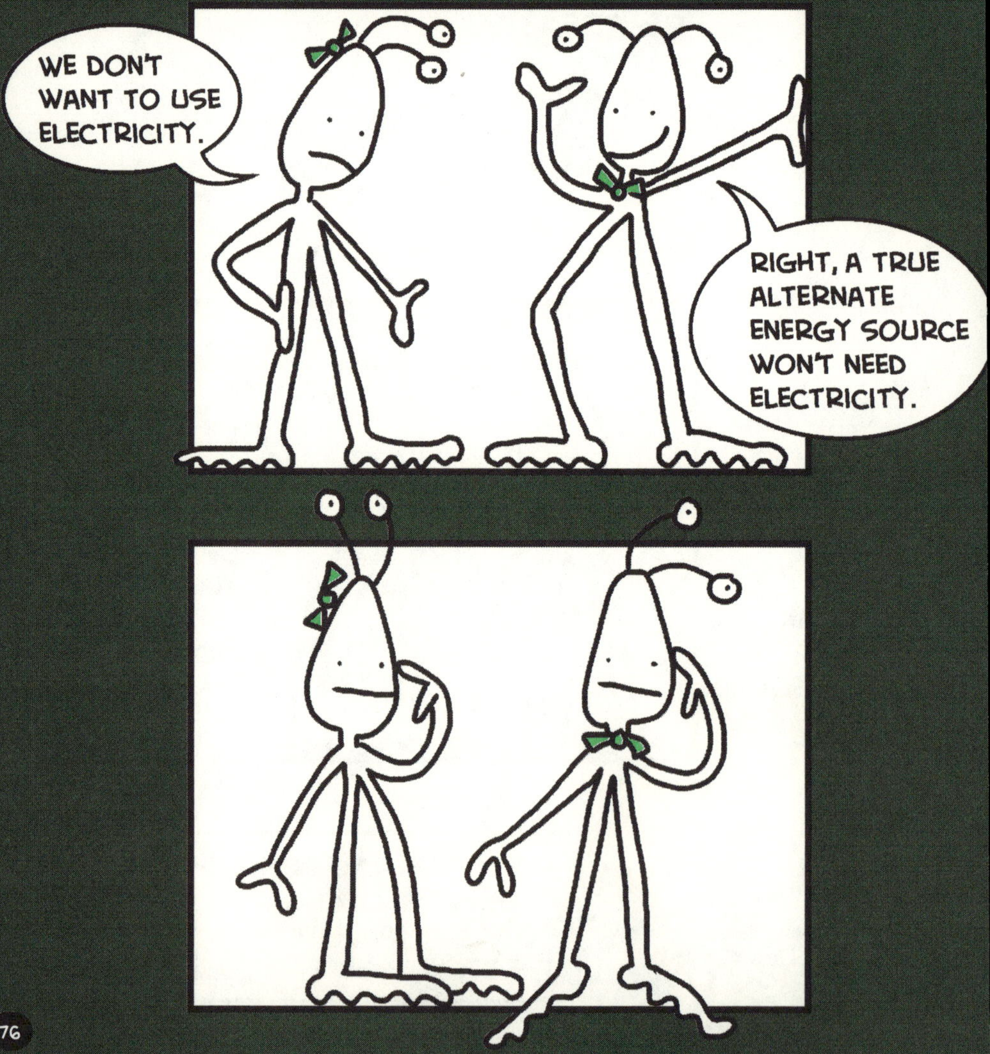
WE DON'T WANT TO USE ELECTRICITY.
RIGHT, A TRUE ALTERNATE ENERGY SOURCE WON'T NEED ELECTRICITY.

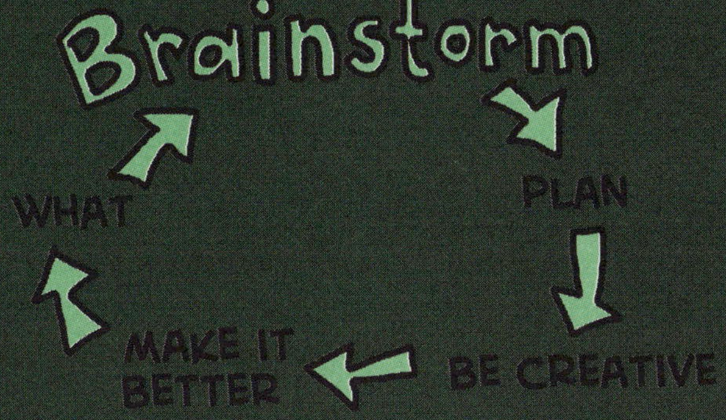
Brainstorm
PLAN
BE CREATIVE
MAKE IT BETTER
WHAT

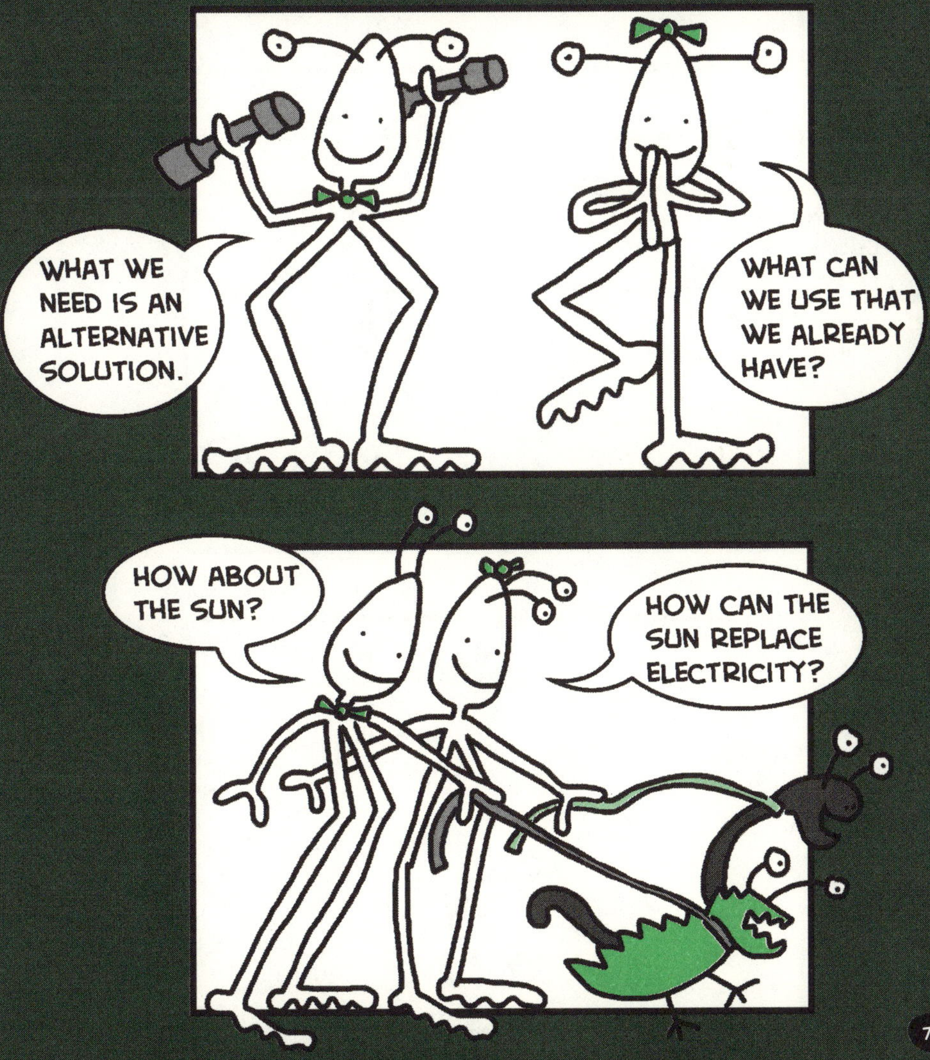
WHAT WE NEED IS AN ALTERNATIVE SOLUTION.
WHAT CAN WE USE THAT WE ALREADY HAVE?
HOW ABOUT THE SUN?
HOW CAN THE SUN REPLACE ELECTRICITY?

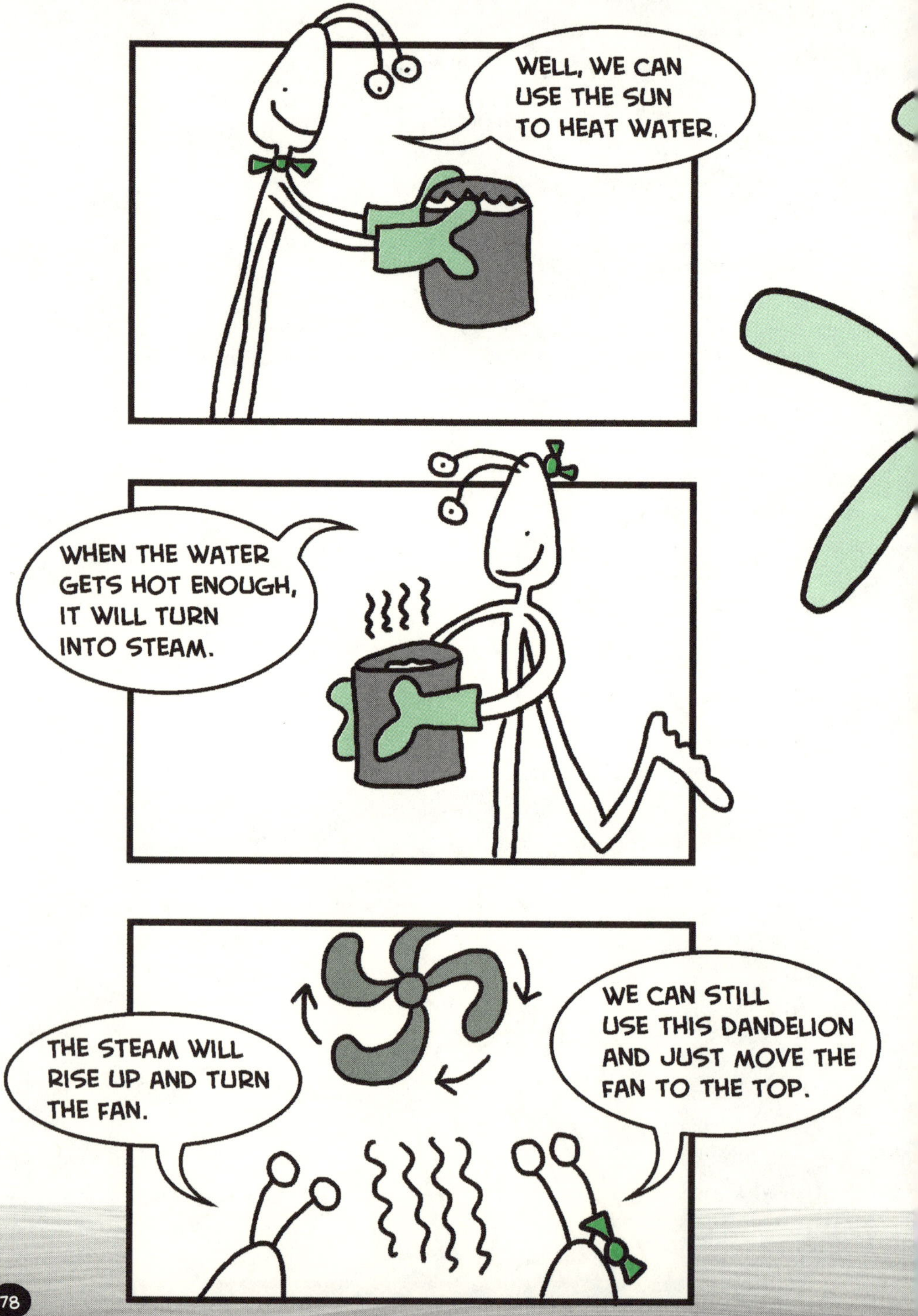
WELL, WE CAN USE THE SUN TO HEAT WATER.
WHEN THE WATER GETS HOT ENOUGH, IT WILL TURN INTO STEAM.
THE STEAM WILL RISE UP AND TURN THE FAN.
WE CAN STILL USE THIS DANDELION AND JUST MOVE THE FAN TO THE TOP.

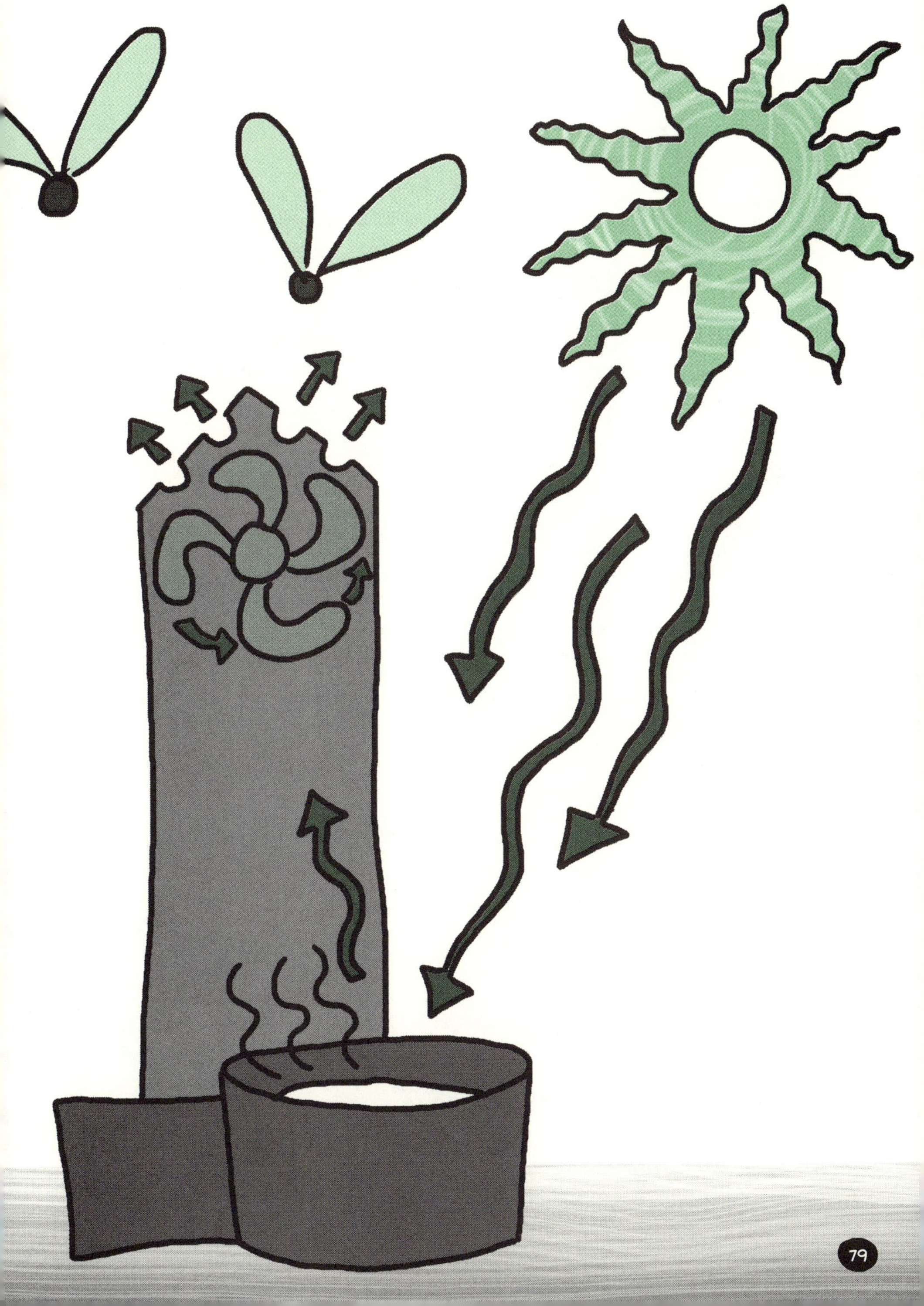

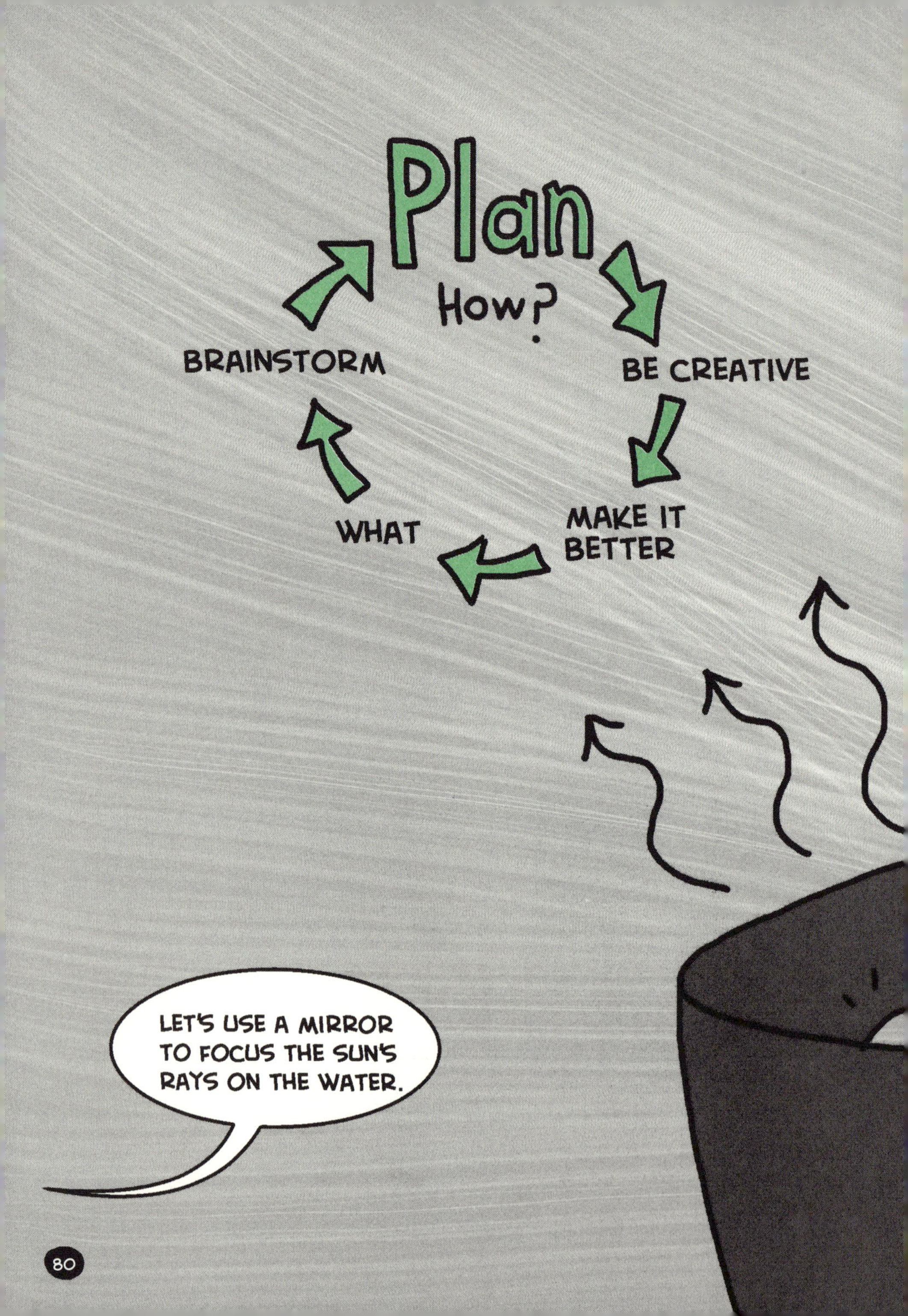
Plan
How?
BE CREATIVE
MAKE IT BETTER
WHAT
BRAINSTORM
LET'S USE A MIRROR TO FOCUS THE SUN'S RAYS ON THE WATER.

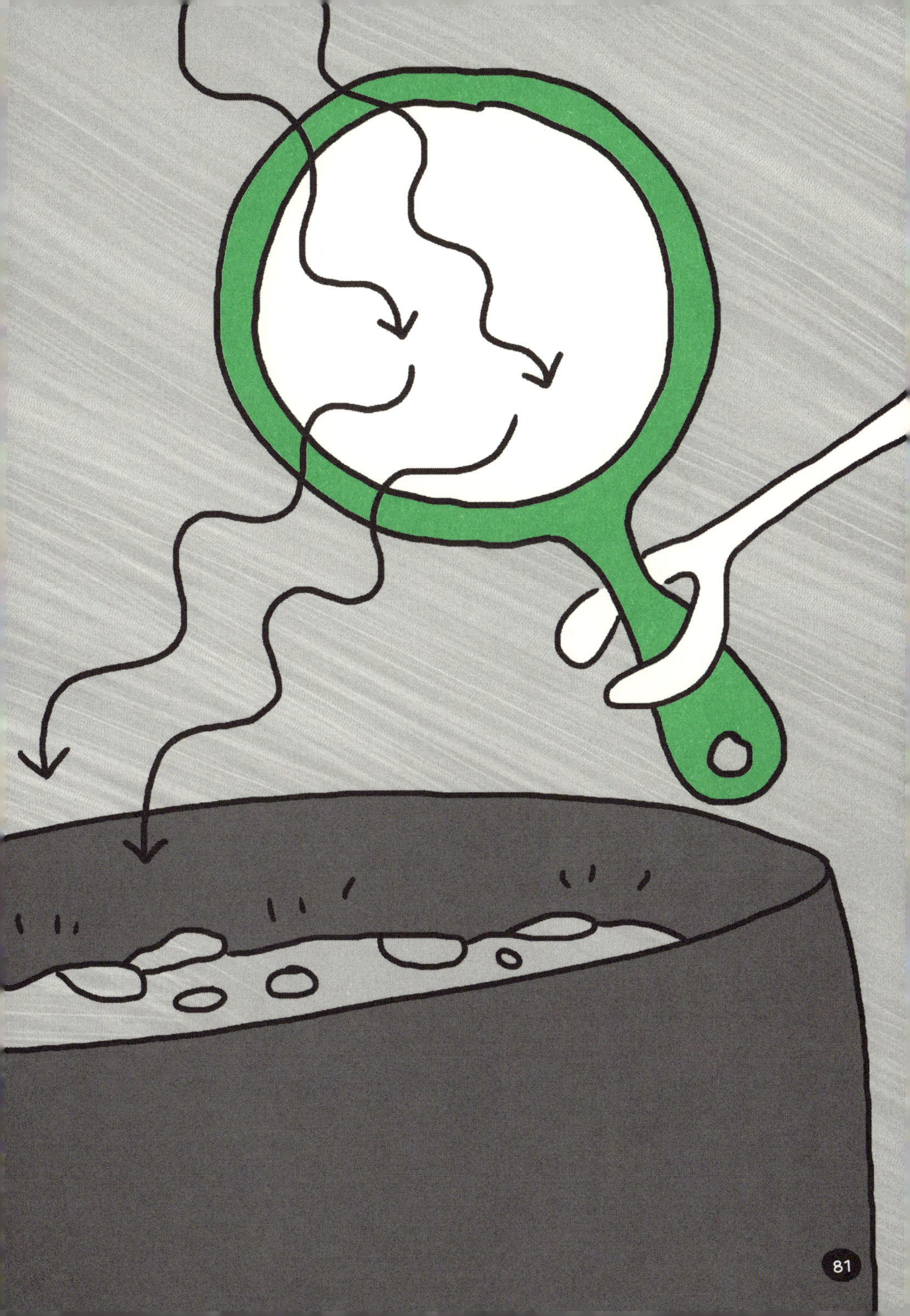

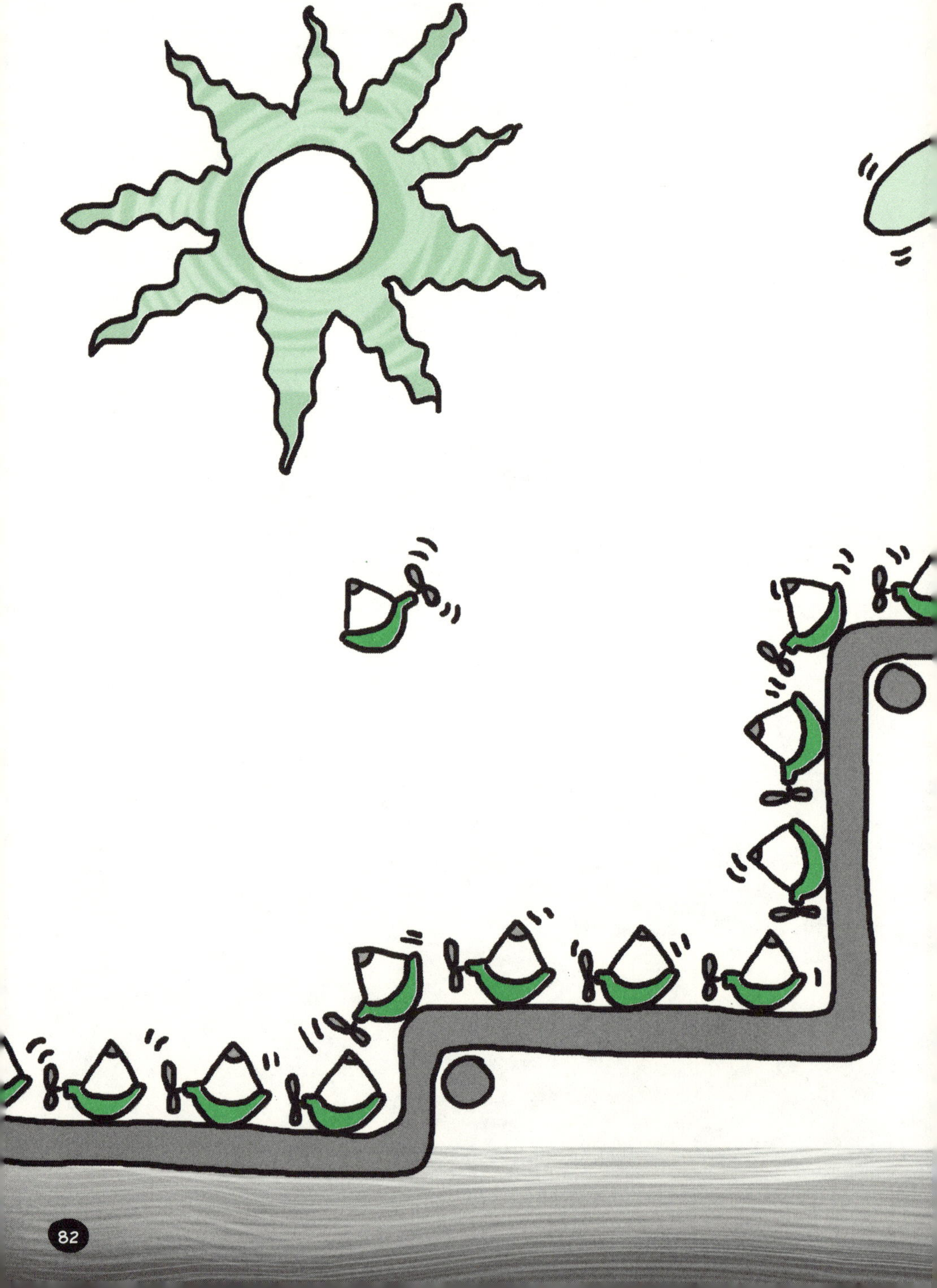

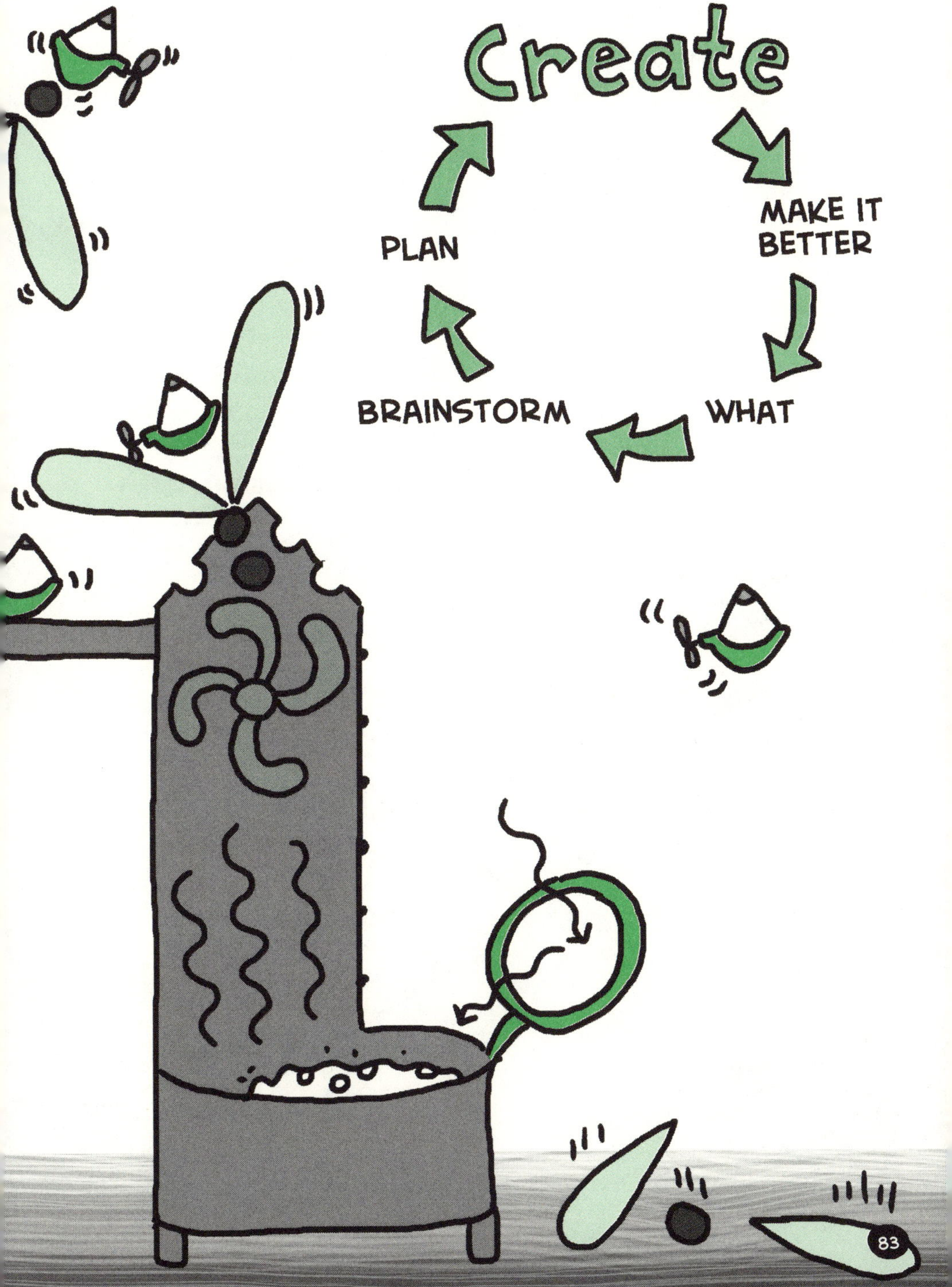
Create
MAKE IT BETTER
WHAT
BRAINSTORM
PLAN

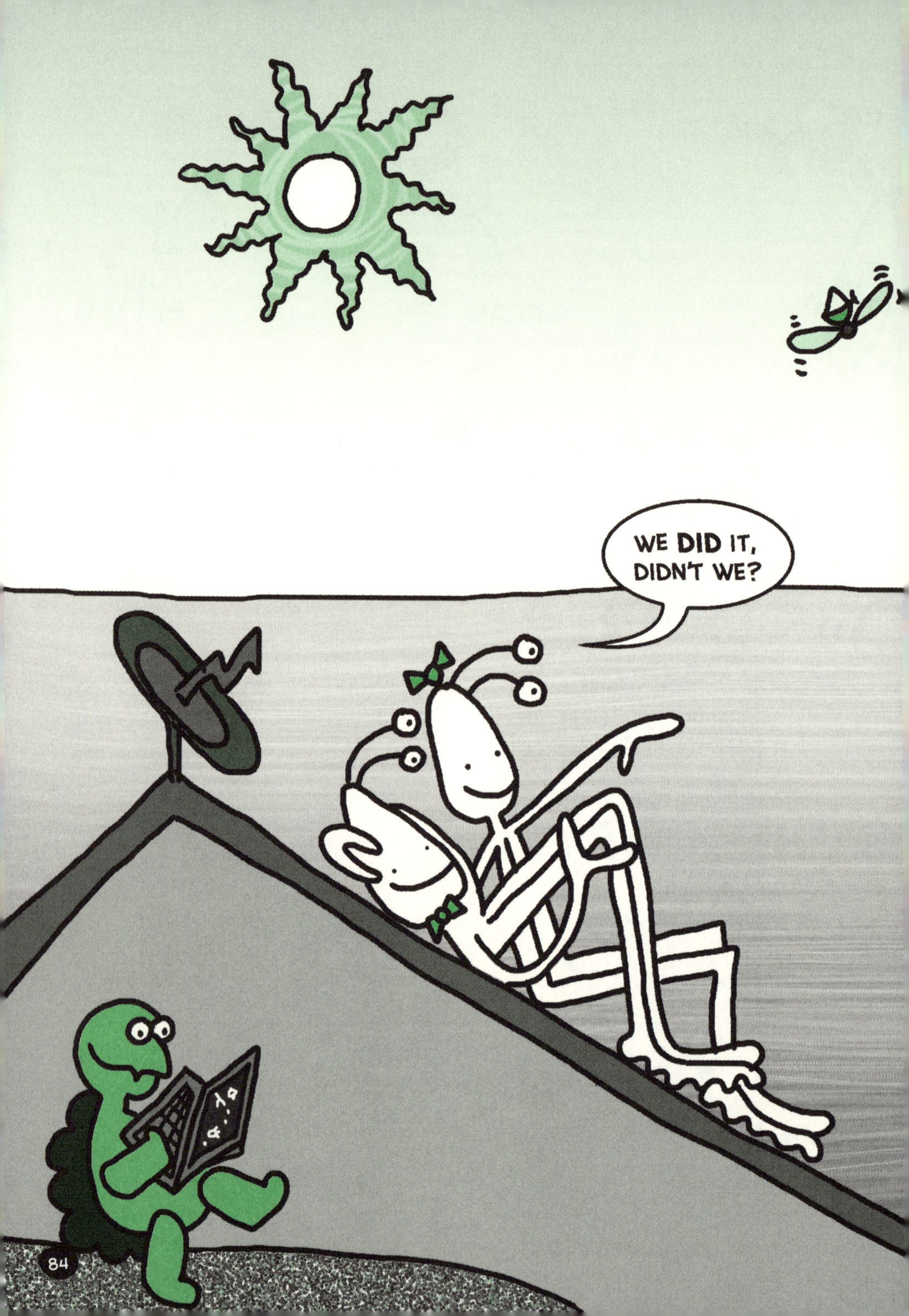
WE DID IT, DIDN'T WE?

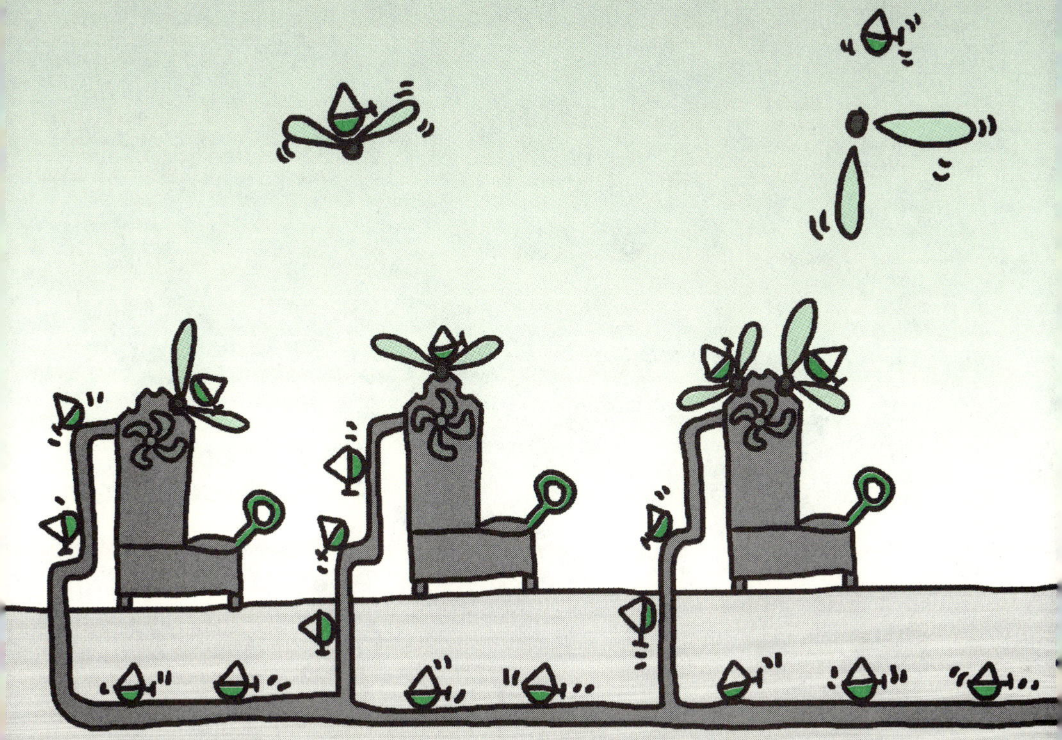

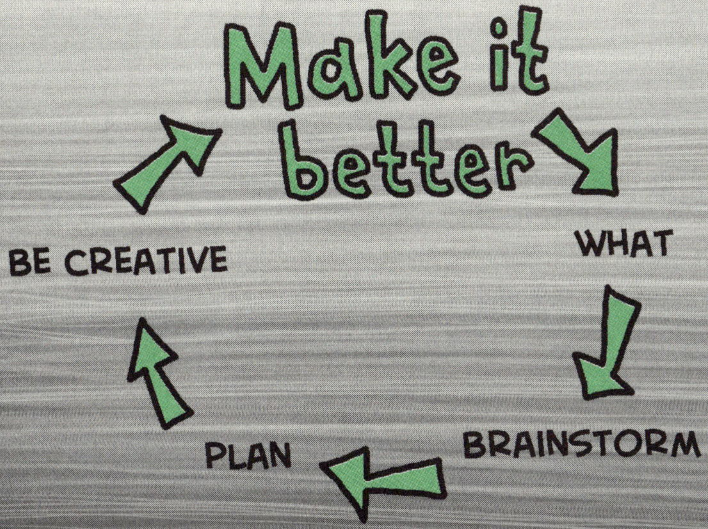
Make it better
WHAT
BRAINSTORM
PLAN
BE CREATIVE

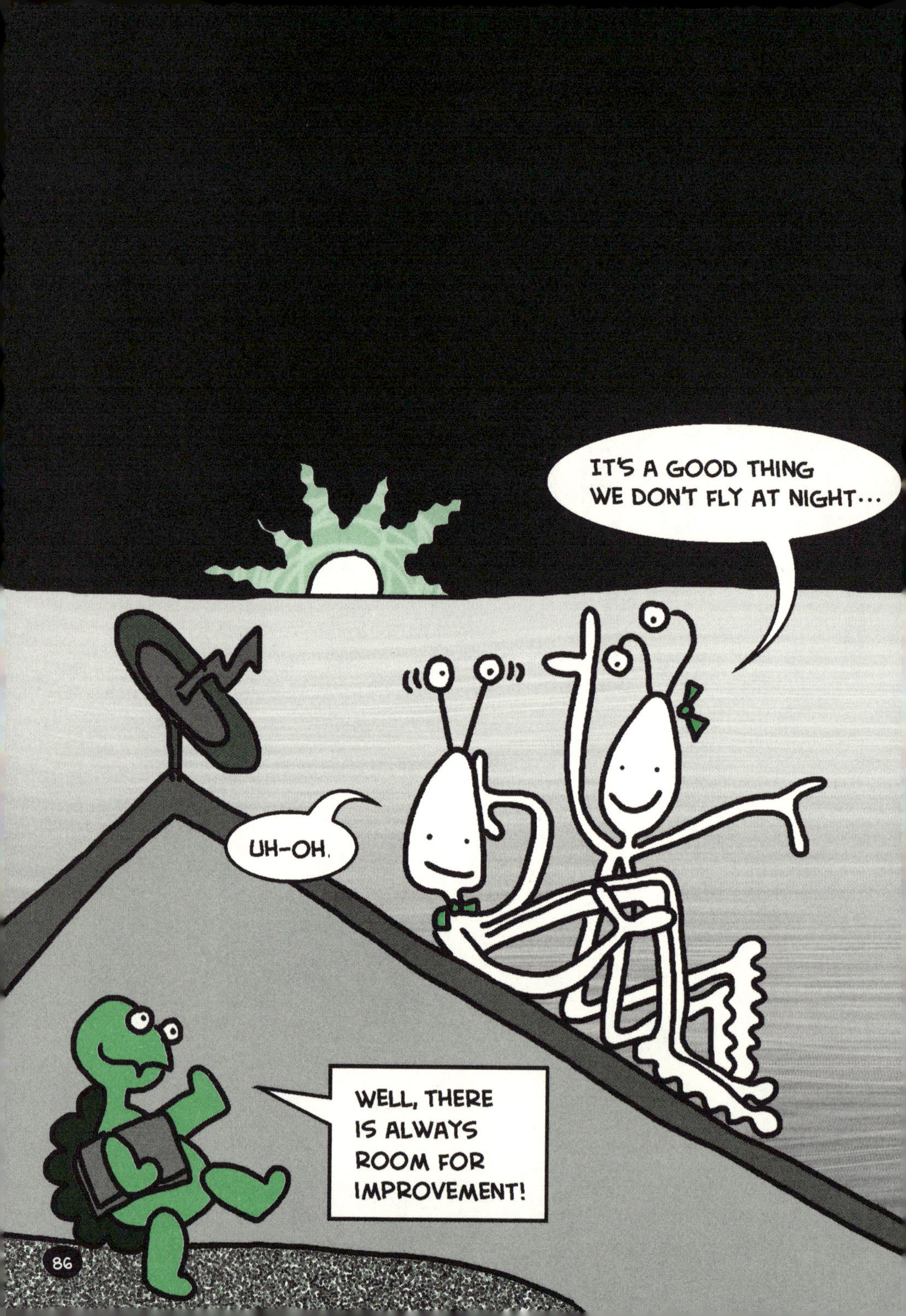
IT'S A GOOD THING WE DON'T FLY AT NIGHT...
UH-OH.
WELL, THERE IS ALWAYS ROOM FOR IMPROVEMENT!

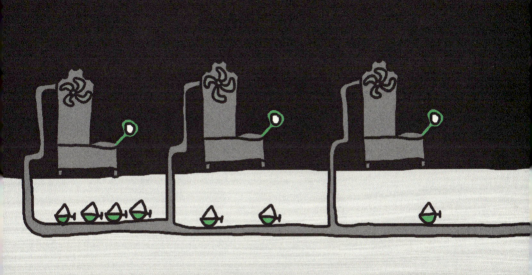

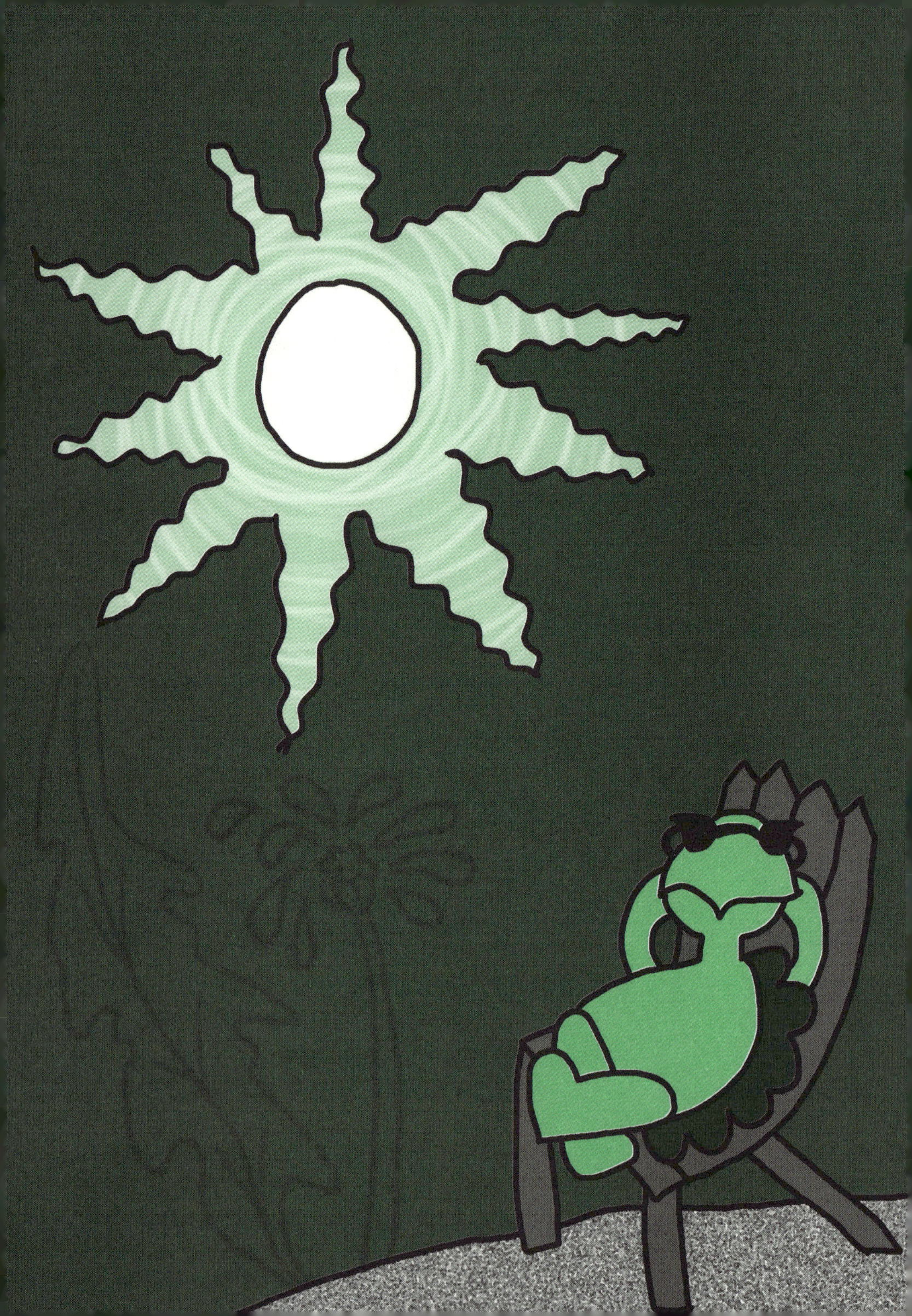

ABOUT THE SERIES:
USING HUMOR, IMAGINATION, AND THE FASCINATION OF DESIGN PROCESS, ENGINEERING EVERYTHING LAUNCHES YOUNG READERS ON PROBLEM-SOLVING ADVENTURES THAT INTRODUCE FUNDAMENTAL SCIENCE, TECHNOLOGY, ENGINEERING, AND MATHEMATICS (STEM) CONCEPTS AND VOCABULARY.

ee
ENGINEERING EVERYTHING

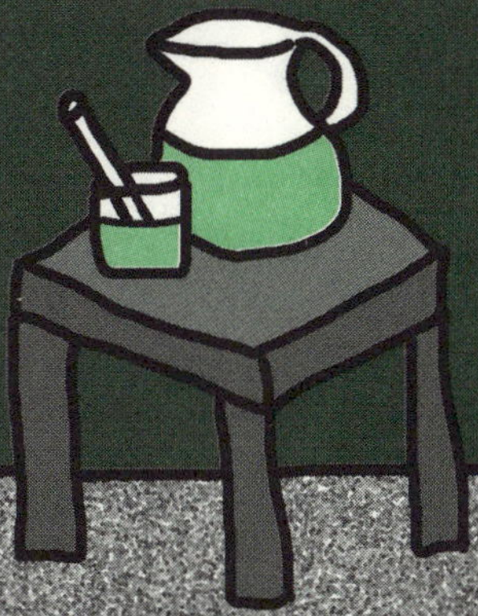

cast of Characters

BELLS

MITCH

ENGINEERING PROFESSOR

MATHEMATICS PROFESSOR

SCIENCE PROFESSOR

TECHNOLOGY PROFESSOR